GET STUFF DONE

THE GSD FACTOR

WORKBOOK

MISHA
BLEYMAIER-FARRISH

GSD
FACTOR \ PUBLISHING

The GSD Factor Workbook
Copyright © 2023 by Misha Bleymaier-Farrish

All rights reserved. This book or any portion thereof may not be reproduced or used
in any manner whatsoever without the express written permission of the publisher
except for the use of brief quotations in a book review.

The name GSD Factor and its visual likeness, including its icon/brand mark,
are property of GSD Factor LLC and protected under trademark law.

Published by
GSD Factor Publishing
www.gsdfactor.com
info@gsdfactor.com
6688 Nolensville Road, Ste. 108-107
Brentwood, TN 37027-8833

Printed in the United States of America

GSD Factor LLC and GSD Factor Publishing LLC are committed to human-generated
content. This book was developed, written, and edited by humans without the
assistance of artificial intelligence.

A special thanks to the GSD Factor Publishing Team:
Book Coach + Editor-in-Chief: Qualia C. Hendrickson
Editor: Alacia Reynolds
Cover Design: Ella Carlton Shirk
Interior Design: Carla Green
Author Headshot: Mat Brown

ISBN 979-8-9877272-4-9 (paperback)

To my fellow GSDers:

Learn something from everything.
Learn what to do, but more importantly, what not to do.
Live authentically.
Be the change makers that you are meant to be.

To: _____

Message: _____

Belongs to: _____

Email: _____

CONTENTS

INTRODUCTION

I was seventeen years old, a senior in high school, sitting with my parents in front of a team of specialists and hearing the words: "We know what's making you sick."

Hearing these words brought a sense of relief and yet fear. For two years, my health had been rapidly declining, and I did not know why. At the age of fifteen, I was a pre-professional dancer, and my fellow dancers were headed to professional dance schools and companies like Julliard and Alvin Alley. I was trying to finish high school as fast as humanly possible because the Royal Ballet of Canada was waiting, but I was struggling, both physically and neurologically. I was barely able to walk, struggling to speak, and even losing my memory. As hard as all that was, the physical ailments weren't even the most difficult thing to swallow. It was the countless doctors and specialists who couldn't figure out my mystery disease and, therefore, jumped to the conclusion that it was all in my head. Up until that point, the only people who believed me were my family.

The next words from the specialists stung even deeper. "You are suffering from Lyme's disease, and you only have three months to live." Talk about a gut punch.

Now, for me, there were only really two options for how to respond: the Bleymaier way and the non-Bleymaier way, and if you know, you know. We Bleymaiers, my family, sprung into action. My health was a problem, and it needed to be solved. If there was a course of action, we did it. If there wasn't a course of action, we created one. There was no problem that a Bleymaier couldn't innovate a solution for.

Back in the late 1990s, Lyme's Disease was a relatively new and unknown disease. If people were diagnosed, it was usually too late. If you found a doctor that did diagnose and treat Lyme's Disease, they were also likely in the throws of research and trailblazing the diagnostics, treatment plans, recovery percentages, you name it. It was uncharted territory for the medical community, and there were so many unknowns surrounding the disease: its effects, potential survival rate, and a patient's quality of life.

The two-year protocol was going to be intense and complex, but now that we knew what the mystery disease was, we could implement a plan or a roadmap to health. My life motto is GSD, or "get stuff done." It is a mentality that ran through my veins from my ancestors before me, ancestors who helped put men on the moon and turned the impossible into the possible. Back then, at seventeen years old, I was in the fight to save my life, and I was going to get that stuff done if it was the last thing I did on this earth.

That journey, though challenging, is only one of many situations that I've faced in my life, situations that pushed me beyond my physical, emotional, and mental limits. Challenges like that have required me to pull from many different places to achieve success. Throughout my life, in those moments, I channel the strength and ingenuity of my family. I refer back to all the lessons my parents taught me, all the times I had been counted out because of gender, age, educational status, or physical impairments. All of these combined experiences ultimately made me who I am—a woman who knows how to get stuff done.

Now, when I say "get stuff done," I'm not trying to coin a catchphrase or hashtag. It's more than that. The GSD Factor ignites a transformation in your life. It's an attitude that helps you accomplish seemingly insurmountable feats. It's a mindset that helps you cultivate an unshakeable confidence in your identity and your abilities. It's about practical execution. I believe that every single one of us has the GSD Factor within us, but maybe, for some of you, it just hasn't been activated or needs to be reignited. Do you consistently find yourself in situations where you feel like an "other" or an "only" because of your gender, age, ethnicity, or simply because you march to the beat of your own drum? Maybe you're a dreamer who's constantly looking for ways to improve. Maybe you're questioning how things have always been. If you inspire others with your resilience or courage and ability to be fully present in all situations, or if you often feel drawn to lead and to use your voice to influence others, then the GSD Factor drive is active in you.

Now that we've established the GSD Factor, here's a little about me. My name is Misha Bleymaier-Farrish. I'm an author, entrepreneur, founder, career coach, speaker, strategic consultant, military-family member, non-profit organization board member, mentor, wife, and mother. I'm an advocate for the under-voiced, mentoring the next generation of leaders and equipping those who may need direction and clarity. As you can tell, I wear many hats. I've been blessed with many talents, and I honor those blessings by making sure I'm operating as efficiently, authentically, smoothly, and purposefully as possible. I get stuff done because I don't want to waste or squander the gifts that have been given to me.

Anyone who knows me, knows that I love to dream big, question the status quo, and just GSD. My team would tell you I'm the GSD boss. My kids would tell you I'm the GSD Momma. Some have even said, about me: "There goes Misha, GSDing!"

Throughout my life, I've always been known as a person who could execute under pressure or otherwise. I realized fairly early that my problem-solving skills and ability to find success in challenging situations didn't come so easily to everyone. I constantly find myself meeting people and almost instantly being asked for advice on a difficult task or problem. My experiences birthed this GSD Factor mindset, and the benefits of GSD Factor living motivate me to share this concept with others.

I know what you're thinking: What is the GSD Factor Life? Why do I need it, and how will having a GSD Factor mindset help me in the future? There are six attributes that come to mind. To live the GSD Factor Lifestyle, you must:

1. Be Confident

2. Be Inquisitive

3. Be Imaginative

4. Be Present

5. Be Resilient

6. Be Influential

Someone with an activated GSD Factor has the confidence or boldness to know their true, authentic self and their own voice and has the assertiveness to speak their truth and be heard. They have the humility to be inquisitive. They ask lots of questions and know that they are not the smartest people in the room, but they have the ability to bring together the right team to ensure that they are open to the fullness of life. They're imaginative or think about things differently and are not afraid to dream big. They're never satisfied with how things have always been done, and say, "I'm here. What can we make better? What is impossible that we can make possible?" They know to be present or be still and trust the process even when it seems that there are more changes than plans. They have the stamina, grit, and perseverance to acknowledge that life can be hard sometimes and the resilience or courage to turn the negatives into positives. Finally, they have influence. They lead by example, look to the future, and bring teammates along with them. These six attributes are the foundational principles from which all other aspects of the GSD Factor develop. They are the attributes that I have cultivated throughout my lifetime and the ones that I find in common with other GSDers I've encountered along my journey.

HOW TO READ AND INTERACT WITH THIS WORKBOOK

Throughout this book, the GSD Factor attributes and the personal lessons from my life's experiences are woven into the chapters. My hope is that these stories will encourage and empower you to activate the GSD Factor within you. I'm not only a strong believer that you can learn something from any experience; I'm walking evidence that it is true. Hopefully, my stories or your own experiences, will provide some guidance on what to do and what not to do.

There are questions, journal prompts, and activities throughout this workbook. These are there to help you think about the GSD Factor attributes and train you on how to use them in your life. You will always need confidence, inquisitiveness, imagination, presence, resilience, and influence. The sooner you learn or reactivate these, the faster you will be able to face anything that life throws at you. You may have already had some struggles, and if that is the case, hopefully these stories and activities will remind you of how awesome you are. Think of it like a high five or a pat on the back. I'm rooting for you. You've got this. I'm so proud of you.

The biggest thing is to connect with other GSDers who are walking your same journey. Share and learn together; laugh and cry, and know you are not alone. I am grateful that you have chosen to embark on this journey with me. Let's stay connected so we can collaborate to harness the power of teamwork, or as we like to say here: Let's GSD! Welcome to your GSD Factor Life.

ATTRIBUTE ONE

BE **CONFIDENT**

Being confident means knowing your true authentic self, knowing your voice, and speaking your truth so that you are heard. You lead by example with assertiveness, giving you a sense of empowerment and confidence.

Obstacles don't have to stop you. If you run into a wall, don't turn around and give up. Figure out how to climb it, go through it, or work around it.

– MICHAEL JORDAN

ACTIVITY

Fill out this sentence:

My name is _____,

and I'm a _____

_____

_____

_____

_____

_____

_____

_____

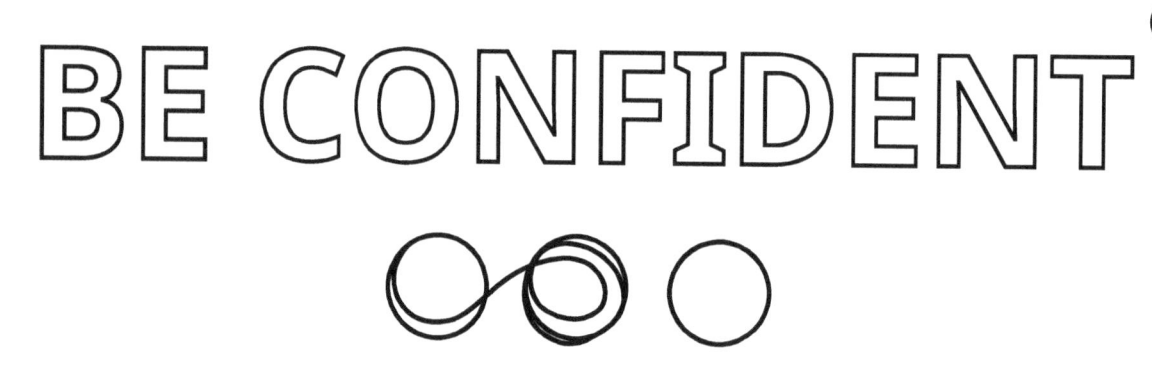

BE CONFIDENT

THE POWER
AND CONFIDENCE
IN KNOWING YOUR
TRUE AUTHENTIC SELF,
KNOWING YOUR VOICE,
AND SPEAKING YOUR TRUTH
SO THAT YOU ARE HEARD.

gsdfactor.com

THIS IS ME

When I was nine, I traveled with my dad to The Frankfurt Book Fair in Germany. Every year, thousands of people attend the week-long event to showcase their latest books and make connections. At the time, Dad was the vice president of international sales for books and music for a contemporary Christian publishing and music company. He attended the fair every year and was an incredible networker. Dad knew how to talk to everyone and had a natural talent for connecting with people, and he could easily spot that same gift in others. Dad would later tell me how he saw that ability to connect with people in me at an early age, especially if they were sick or injured. Instances like that showed him that I not only had a special concern for helping people, but I also had a confidence that gave me the boldness and courage to talk to anyone. Looking back at it, I believe that he must have specifically taken me on this trip to ignite that confidence in me.

On this particular trip, he saw my sales and networking potential and decided to give me an opportunity to hone that skill set. My job was to read every new release that we were showcasing and be able to tell people about it. Sounds pretty easy, right? Maybe for an adult who had years of training and experience in sales, but I was nine! Still, even at nine years old, I knew that if I didn't put myself out there, I wouldn't make the connections that I needed. Dad knew that, too, and he prepared me for how to engage with people. We prepared talking points for each book. He taught me to make eye contact, smile, and then speak so that people would come into my booth and want to learn more. Dad also prepared me for rejection by telling me that it was a normal thing. He emphasized that I would have to get through a "no" to get to a "yes," and I quickly realized that the faster you get through the "no," the better!

That day, I made my way around to the other booths, introducing myself and getting to know the neighbors. I talked about the books Dad brought and whatever else I could think of. Thankfully, I had my dad's gift of gab, so the conversation flowed freely. I was definitely the only kid there. Looking back on the experience, I can see how I naturally realized the importance of connecting with people. It's not hard to find commonalities with people; it just takes effort. I was able to engage with people and navigate those interactions effortlessly. Even if I was faced with a no, I went back one more time to see if I could win them over. If I could, great! If I couldn't, it was okay because it was great interaction practice.

Fast forward to my present-day life, and we can see the impact this early experience had on me. I've never been afraid to talk to people, go to an event where I knew no one, or try new things. My experience at the Frankfurt Book Fair is one of those memories that will stay with me for the rest of my life, and it is one of the moments that helped shape who I am.

Working at the book fair gave me an early glimpse of what I would later discover to be the Get Stuff Done Factor, or GSD Factor for short. That nine-year-old girl learned what it meant to be confident and comfortable in her own skin and how to leverage that confidence to connect with people. I couldn't put a name to it then, but I know now that this trip helped shape my assertiveness, dedication, and my voice. I tip my hat to my dad and thank him for those skill sets that he taught me at such a young age.

ACTIVITY

What gifts do you have? How can you turn those gifts into assets in your life?

GIFT	ASSET

A SPACE TO DREAM BIG . . .

A SPACE TO DREAM BIG . . .

YOUR TRUE AUTHENTIC SELF

You are a unicorn. This is one of the fundamental points to remember when we start to think about what the GSD Factor is. What does this mean? Why a unicorn?

I'm a mom to two great kids, and my husband and I are always looking for books and tools that can help them and us as we navigate parenting in this day and age. One of our favorite tools is called Slumberkins, an organization dedicated to helping families raise caring, confident, and resilient children through affirmations, stories, and creature characters. Slumberkins have developed these amazing characters and turned them into stuffed animals with beautifully written stories meant to encourage children's emotional growth. Their story of the unicorn is one that shows tiny humans the power of authenticity, and it promotes this alongside bravery and friendship. The story's protagonist is the unicorn, who is unique and authentic but wants to fit in so badly with her new friends, the zebras. Throughout the story, she changes her look and the way she acts in a desperate attempt to conform to her peers. She misses the fact that she is losing herself in the process. She doesn't realize that what makes her unique is tied to her identity. It's her true, authentic self. This story is a creative way to teach kids confidence and self-acceptance, but the lesson is universal across all ages. The first GSD Factor attribute of being confident is directly related to this idea of the unicorn and embracing authenticity. Being confident and assertive about who you are and your beliefs are the fuel that propels one to action. GSDers celebrate uniqueness because we understand that differences cultivate stronger teams, families, and organizations. Diversity creates an atmosphere for endless possibilities, so being a unicorn–distinct, authentic, irreplicable–is an asset and a tell-tale sign of a person who gets stuff done.

So many times, we find ourselves conforming to those around us. We change our look because that's what the celebrities and social media tell us to do. We change how we speak and what we say because it's what everyone else is doing or has done. We make ourselves smaller so we can blend with the crowd. How much more interesting would life be if, instead of changing our looks, personalities, and voices to fit in, we amplified the unique aspects of ourselves to enhance and enrich those around us? If we embraced being the unicorn? What if we used our peculiarities to tell a different story, a unicorn story, a GSD Factor story? Sure, our voice can still be heard in a choir, but when we step forward into the spotlight, looking, sounding, and acting a little differently, our voice is not only heard but remembered.

When I was approached about writing my first book by a major publisher, I thought they were crazy. I was recovering from professional corporate burnout. I had just founded my first company, Etymology Consulting, and my tiny humans were tiny. I literally laughed out loud to the publisher. But their suggestion intrigued me enough to have additional conversations and to make a trip to their corporate offices.

As I sat there in the conference room (which ironically carried the same name as my oldest tiny human), I was hearing their words, and the want and desire to write a book was igniting, but perhaps not the way they were outlining, not the way that all their other authors had done it before.

You see, I am a unicorn and I wanted to write my own words, own my material, publish on my own timeline, and keep my name. Why? Because this was me being my unapologetically true, authentic self. If I didn't do these things, how could I publish or speak to The GSD Factor Life if I hadn't lived it myself.

My sister had accompanied me to the myriad of meetings, and afterward, we proceeded to debrief with our bourbons overlooking the ocean. I'll never forget her words. She said, "You are meant to write a book. Write away! The world needs your ideas. But this is not the GSD way. You will find and make your own path."

The question I have for you is this: Are you a unicorn, or are you a zebra? Being a unicorn embodies the GSD Factor and builds that muscle of confidence each time you choose to stand boldly in your true, authentic self. Being confident becomes much easier when you are consistently embracing all of the differences and unique qualities that make you who you are. It's simple. The more you show up as your true self, the more assertive you can be in challenging and difficult situations.

Be confident in who you are, and don't diminish yourself to make others comfortable. This is your life, and the more you embrace your uniqueness, the more empowered you will feel and become. That's when you can really start to get stuff done!

ACTIVITY

Set a timer for 60 seconds and write all the things you like about yourself.

_____

_____

_____

_____

Set another timer for 60 seconds and write all the things you dislike about yourself.

_____

_____

_____

_____

Which list is longer? _____

Are the things you don't like about yourself flaws or uniqueness? It's important to distinguish between the two. Have you been viewing your uniqueness as a disadvantage/flaw? Use the space below to reflect:

The things we like, dislike, and consider different about ourselves contribute to who we are as a whole. Acknowledging those things and either deciding to accept, capitalize, or change them are all parts of embracing your true, authentic self. Look at your lists again. First, really consider whether your dislikes are actually flaws or just unique traits.

Use the chart below to write out the perceived flaws, and in the column across from it, write the opposite of the flaw.

FLAW	OPPOSITE

Consider ways that you can evolve or improve upon the things you wrote in both columns and the ways that these traits make you unique. List at least three ways you can use your "uniqueness" to your advantage.

A SPACE TO DREAM BIG . . .

USE YOUR VOICE

My parents raised me and my sister with gratitude for what we were blessed with and with a spirit of giving to those less fortunate than ourselves. After my dad retired from the music and book publishing industry, he began working for non-profit organizations in the fundraising sector. He and my mom ran fundraising golf tournaments for organizations such as Habitat for Humanity, Young Life, and the Kidney Foundation. Their biggest focus, no matter who they were fundraising for, was to tell a story and to make an emotional connection. Dad knew that sharing stories would create more empathy from potential donors and motivate them to give. Additionally, if the story really resonated with the donors, they would be more likely to share those stories with others and subsequently help spread awareness about whatever particular cause the organization was championing. Over his fourteen-year career in nonprofit fundraising, Dad helped to raise over $10 million dollars. Watching my parents use their voices to raise funds for these organizations gave me a front-row seat to see how impactful we can be when we use our voices and influence to advocate for good.

Over the years, fundraising has taught me many lessons. It boosted my confidence in my ability to connect with people and have meaningful conversations. Most importantly, it showed me the power of my voice and the potential it has to reach the multitude. Your network may be small, but you never know how it can amplify. You may only tell one person, but it may be the RIGHT one person. Sometimes, when we use our voice, even to the few people around us, it can have a snowball effect that can reach millions around the world.

Both my kids are in martial arts and, along with training their bodies, their Sensei teaches his students character-building lessons. The first and most valuable lesson they learn is that their voice is their strongest weapon. For each of my kids to have heard, at the age of four, that their voice is their strongest weapon was a day of empowerment that they hadn't experienced before. They both felt unstoppable. And that lesson will stay with them for the rest of their lives.

Research shows us that positive words can actually change one's brain and restructure it. Let's ponder this for a moment. If positive words can change one's brain structure, is it safe to assume that negative words, reinforced over and over again, are actually changing our brain waves as well? We aren't living in the most positive time, and I, wholeheartedly believe we have restructured our brains. The impact this is having on governments, responses to pandemics, wars, etc. is troubling. We have been feeding our brains and the universe with negative energy. We have to stop.

Let's look at this in our world today. We deserve to live in positivity. It has to start with you and me speaking more positively within our personal and professional lives and the community around us. Our children deserve to grow up in a world where positivity is more the norm, especially because everyone isn't vibrating at the same level of positivity and kindness. But positivity is not something that has an instant fix, and some prefer the instant gratification of negativity.

When we were kids, we knew these people as bullies. Both my tiny humans have been targeted by fellow classmates and bullied both verbally and, eventually, physically. As their mother, I want to ensure that they are ready and trained in the art of verbal warfare. Our voice is our strongest weapon, and we should use it. We should use it for good. Use it to build up. Use it for innovation, ideas, and exploration. Use it to protect and advocate.

In both cases with my tiny humans, not only did we equip them with the words to say directly to their bully, but also to speak up and tell the teacher or staff. My husband and I used our own voices to escalate and raise the issue with the appropriate leadership. We raised our voices because we were standing up for our tiny humans, but also the other tiny humans in the classes, and yes, even the bully themselves. We had two very different responses. One leadership team heard us, thanked us for bringing it to their attention in such a constructive way, and proceeded to make changes in the school district by implementing education, awareness, training, and advocacy. The other response was not so positive. The other leadership team refused to speak with us, citing privacy policies. On multiple occasions, they didn't report the physical assault of our child to us ahead of us picking them up with visible injuries or hearing our child's account of the incidents firsthand. They eventually—and appallingly—dismissed us from the school because we were causing "too much disruption" and we were "triggering the bully and bully behavior." This "leadership" team told us it was our tiny human's fault for bringing this upon themselves. Unsurprisingly, the bully did not stop and simply redirected their aggression at other children in the classroom.

In both situations, there is nothing we would have done differently when speaking up for our children. Both our tiny humans acknowledged as much and thanked us. They told us they felt heard and that they knew they could share anything with us. Most importantly, they felt safe and continue to feel safe with us. They saw us take action and stand up and defend them. This gave them the confidence and courage to stand up for themselves and others. It's not uncommon that I will hear from teachers and coaches that my tiny humans have stood up to other bullies or protected other vulnerable kids. When asked why they did that, they said, "Our voice is our strongest weapon. Our parents have shown us how they use their voices, and they have taught us to use our voices for ourselves and for others."

However, bullying is not just an adolescent struggle. There are grown, adult bullies in our workplaces, leading, teaching, you name it. If you are not speaking about life, hope, and encouragement, you need to reconsider what you are saying. If you make fun of someone's clothes or hair, you are a bully. If you question their life choices—which is exactly that, a life choice—you are a bully. If you believe yourself superior to everyone else and believe that you are protected and absolved, you are a bully.

Words do hurt, and if you've spent any time in the workforce, you can attest to the fact that people can say some hurtful things to and about you at work. I have had negative experiences with both men and women in professional environments who have used their voices to tear me and others down.

For the sake of the next generation, I want to address what we can do. We have talked previously about the use of our voice as the strongest weapon and the hyper-importance of speaking positivity into the world. We have always taught our kids that life has both choices and consequences. We have taught them that we are to show kindness, love, and respect to each individual in the world. Even when we don't agree.

Be a kind, adult human. Evaluate your life, your words, your choices. Think about what your new life would look like with a positive outlook, having a "there is always something to learn from every experience in life" outlook and echoing that perspective in the words you use. That's living The GSD Factor Life and using your voice for good. We all have a choice in the words we speak, so let's take that sentiment to heart and speak words of life, power, and positivity.

ACTIVITY

How have you used your voice as a weapon? Be honest here without fear of judgment. Have you used it to harm or to help? If the answer is "to harm," what could you have done differently to use your voice in a positive way? If you consistently use your voice to help, how do you ensure that you continue down that same path, even in the face of adversity?

_____

_____

_____

_____

_____

_____

_____

_____

_____

A SPACE TO DREAM BIG . . .

A SPACE TO DREAM BIG . . .

A SPACE TO DREAM BIG . . .

7

PASSION AND DEDICATION

Everything up until this point has been about who you are and how you show up in the world. We've discussed the importance of being confident and brave; embracing your true, authentic self; and using your voice to empower yourself and others. All of these qualities play an important part in living the GSD Factor life. Now let's talk about passion and dedication and how they fit into this puzzle. What's the difference between passion and dedication?

Passion is the GSD Factor attribute that equates to the fire in your belly to get stuff done. It's the love of something so deep that you can't imagine not doing it. If asked to sacrifice something for your passion, there is zero hesitation. It comes to you as natural as breathing. You go to sleep thinking about it. You dream about it, and in the morning, you have fresh ideas about it. Your passion does not feel like work to you. No matter how tough life is, you show up. You dig deep for it. You are striving to improve it, to be the best you can be.

Dedication is the GSD Factor attribute that serves as the grit and the stamina driving your passion to the point of excellence and greatness. It's the drive in your life that says one sport, one after-school activity or one passion is not enough. It's the drive that says studying and training on the bare minimum is settling. It's the attitude that consistently goes above and beyond, arrives early, and stays late, even on weekends. It's also the wisdom to know when to rest and recharge.

I think passion and dedication are the things that you rely on, even if you aren't sure of your direction or path. They're the things that you fall back on in those moments when your future is uncertain, especially when you are walking down a path that others intend to use to hurt you, push you out, or ruin your reputation.

One of the most poignant memories I have of a time when my passion and dedication to my profession were challenged was when I had just returned from one of my maternity leaves. After almost three years of making improvements to streamline some of the processes, I returned to a company that suddenly treated me with extreme hostility and blatant disrespect. I am convinced, to this day, that it was all as a result of my pregnancy. Everything had been going fine until I announced that I was pregnant. Before my pregnancy, I had led trailblazing initiatives that propelled the company forward in the insurance, technology, and financial institution space. During my pregnancy, I had completed a two-year transition of our Salesforce CRM from the classic environment to the lightning environment. CRM, or "customer relationship management," systems are what companies use to manage and analyze customers' data and interactions. My approach, planning, execution, and leadership, which successfully transitioned our organization that had been running Salesforce for over twelve years, was so creative and innovative that I was invited to speak at the Salesforce annual Dreamforce conference that same year. I was invited to host a roundtable discussion with twelve executives in their Success Lodge and share the successes and failures of our organization's transformation. Given the hostility I was facing in the workplace due to my pregnancy, I was unsure how Salesforce would react to my announcement, but they welcomed the news with enthusiasm and excitement. This is a huge testament to the world-class act that Salesforce is. Not only did they recognize and honor me as a trailblazer in my industry, but they amplified and celebrated me as a mom in tech.

Those early weeks after I returned from my maternity leave, it was my grit and determination that said this will not be the thing that takes me down. My dedication and tenacity were on overdrive. Each day was a battle to look for the joy in staying. Each day was a test, another story that I could share with other moms who had experienced what I had experienced. Each day was me walking out the GSD Factor for myself, my family, my colleagues, and, especially, for those who did these hurtful things to me. I kept showing up each and every day, and it drove them crazy. Some said to me, "Why don't you leave? It's embarrassing. I'm embarrassed for you." Others said, "You should file a discrimination case." Even the hotline and my lawyers advised me to do so, but I waited and still showed up. I was patient.

I wanted to prove that workplace bullies would not win. You might strip someone of their roles and responsibilities, remove them from the executive floor, or uninvite them from every meeting so there is nothing on their calendar. You can take away any and everything from the GSDer in the organization, but the truth remains. My passion and dedication for operational and technology excellence and for getting stuff done even when the headwinds were strong won out. I decided I would leave on my own terms and not because imposter syndrome ran through the executive team with whom I previously worked.

Passion and dedication are powerful forces to be reckoned with, and once you know your passion and what you're dedicated to, you gain even more confidence. That increase in confidence makes it much easier to be comfortable with your uniqueness and authenticity, as well as your ability to use your voice. Can you see how all of this works together? Passion and dedication are especially powerful when you are certain about them both. You can run one without the other, but when you run with both, it's nuclear. It's life changing. The energy behind it makes people speechless.

ACTIVITY

Let's practice introducing ourselves and sharing a little bit about our story. Stand in front of a mirror or find a friend to practice role play with. This 1 minute elevator pitch is critical to make contact and be remembered.

A SPACE TO DREAM BIG . . .

ACTION PLAN

HOW TO BE CONFIDENT

Be confident or be bold. The sentence is simple, but the concept is rather complex. This first, and possibly most important GSD Factor attribute is composed of three smaller keys: Knowing and embracing your true authentic self, using your voice, and finding your passion and dedication.

With individuals who want to improve their confidence and assertiveness, I tend to recommend role play, coaching, or even acting classes. When faced with a difficult situation or conversation, role-playing can be an effective way to prepare for every scenario. My mom and dad did it with me all throughout my life, and it has worked. You can do this alone or with your mentor, friends, or family members. Whatever the circumstance, role-playing allows you to practice the tone, volume, and authority of your voice.

Here are three steps for role-playing:

1. Think about the situation or conversation, and write out all of the possible scenarios that could develop, including the opposing side of things. This will give you an opportunity to have a response ready for a variety of comments. You can't predict the future, but this will bolster your confidence as you prepare for the conversation. You won't feel like you're going into the situation blind.

2. Get with a mentor or friend and talk through every scenario that you listed. It is helpful to work with a teammate because you will have real-time feedback on the quality and effectiveness of your arguments and comments.

3. In addition to practicing with a mentor or friend, it is also helpful to practice in the mirror. This will make you aware of your body language and facial expressions. If you're confident in how you look, you'll be more confident in what you are saying. You would be surprised how helpful this can be.

ACTIVITY

We just practiced role play in the mirror or with a friend. Now let's reflect on the power of body language and facial expressions:

Stand in front of a mirror and observe your body language and facial expressions. What do you notice? How does your body language impact your confidence? What does your body language communicate? Do you see your full self reflected?

Write about the importance of confident, non-verbal communication and how practicing in front of a mirror can improve your overall assertiveness.

_____

_____

_____

_____

_____

Flip back to any of the activities throughout this chapter and read your answers out loud confidently. Try different expressions, stances, postures. Find the best for you and practice. Additionally, consider revisiting these activities on a regular cadence, quarterly or twice yearly. The practical application of the GSD Factor attributes will evolve over time as you transform and grow in your professional and personal life.

A Mantra for Being Confident

I know who I am.

I am confident.

I am bold.

I embrace my true, authentic self.

I do not apologize for being me.

I use my voice for myself.

I use my voice for others.

I am passionate.

I am dedicated.

See me.

Hear me.

Know me.

I know who I am.

A SPACE TO DREAM BIG . . .

ATTRIBUTE TWO

BE INQUISITIVE

Being inquisitive is about having the capacity to always be learning, ever a student of life; to walk in humility knowing that you are not the smartest person in the room but know how to mobilize the right team and people; to ensure that you are open to the fullness of life.

The greatest thing about tomorrow is, I will be better than I am today...There is no such thing as a setback. The lessons I learned today I will apply tomorrow, and I will be better.

– TIGER WOODS

ACTIVITY

List some of your favorite ways of learning new things. Are you a visual learner? Do you need to see it to learn it? Are you an auditory learner? Do you need to hear about it? Or are you a kinesthetic learner, someone who actually has to do/experience it to learn? Knowing your preferred learning style can help you determine what kinds of questions to ask as you remain in a state of inquisitiveness.

_____

_____

_____

_____

_____

_____

_____

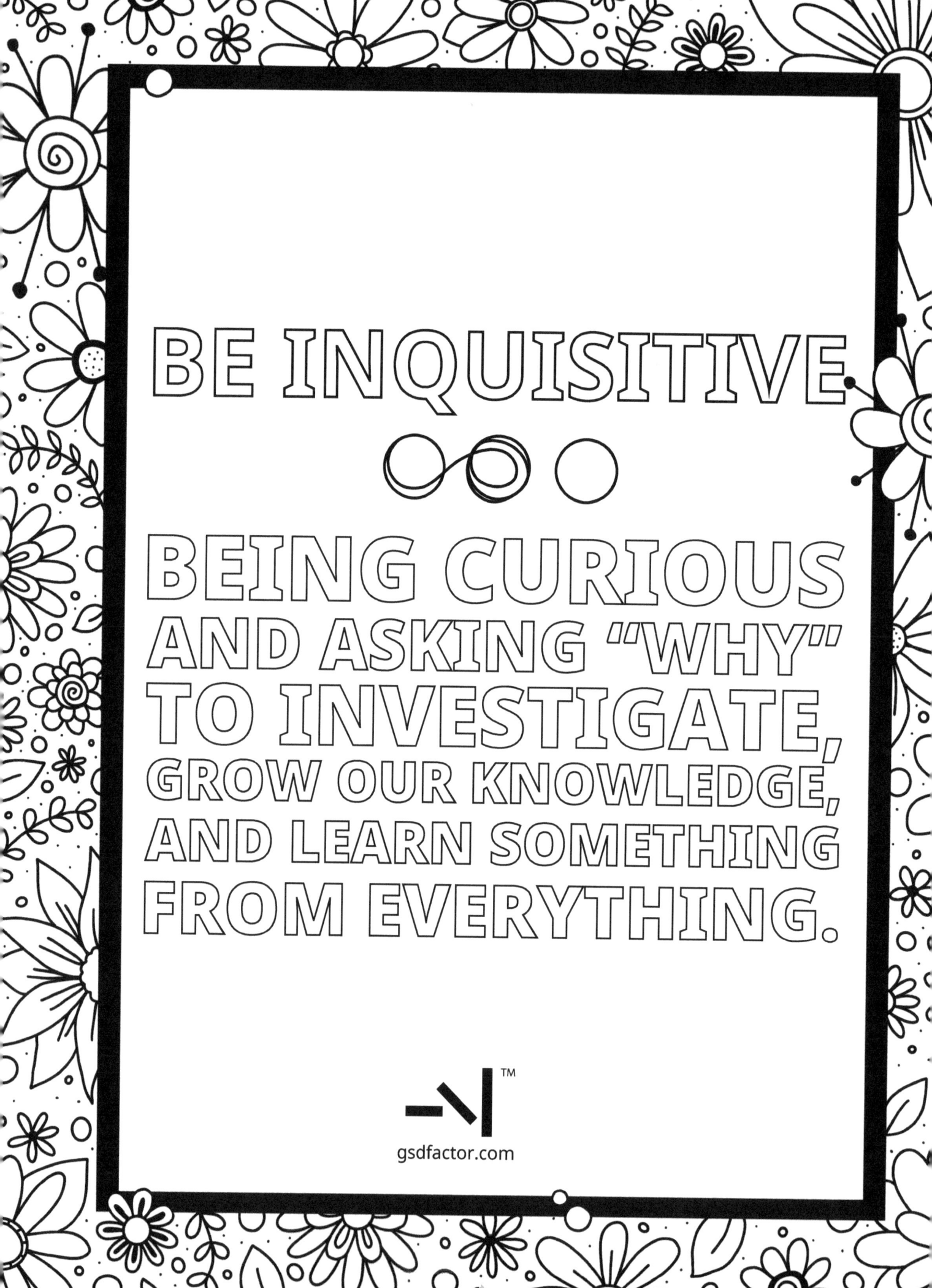

BE INQUISITIVE

BEING CURIOUS AND ASKING "WHY" TO INVESTIGATE, GROW OUR KNOWLEDGE, AND LEARN SOMETHING FROM EVERYTHING.

gsdfactor.com

ALWAYS LEARN SOMETHING

There aren't many things that I know to be absolutes in this world. However, I do know at least one absolute fact: no one person knows everything. Even though there may not be one source to reference for all of life's questions, I'm a firm believer that you can learn something from every experience, whether it's your own experience or something you hear along the way that can make an impact. There are many places from where we can learn things: podcasts, books, workshops, seminars. Overall, great learning can be gleaned by observing others.

This second GSD Factor attribute is based on being inquisitive – being curious, asking questions, soliciting the knowledge and wisdom of others. I think one of the most underutilized learning tools is asking questions: of others and of yourself.

In season one of *Ted Lasso*, there is a great scene in the pub with characters Ted and Rupert playing darts. The scene is set with Ted playing with his non-dominant hand. Rupert immediately assumes that Ted can't play darts. A wager is agreed upon, and before long Ted starts playing with his dominant hand while waxing eloquent about a quote he had seen: "Be curious, not judgemental." The lesson that Ted not only talks about but demonstrates in a GSD Factor manner is that you can never underestimate someone. Instead, you need to be curious, asking questions because you will learn something. The trick is not learning something too late. Had Rupert been curious about him and not judgmental, the lesson he would have learned was that Ted, who ultimately won the wager on the final throw, was actually an excellent dart player.

This less than two-minute scene of television encapsulates so many great nuggets of wisdom that can be applied to The GSD Factor Life. Lesson number one is to ask questions and be curious. When you ask, you learn. You can be learning about someone else, a team, an organization, or yourself. Lesson number two is don't make assumptions, and certainly, don't be judgemental. Part of the definition of inquisitiveness is knowing you are not the smartest person in the room. You can't walk in humility while being an assumptive and judgemental human. A common English idiom is, "Don't judge a book by its cover." The same certainly holds true for humans, especially in this ever-changing DEIB (Diversity, Equity, Inclusion, and Belonging) world. Lesson number three is don't underestimate. Don't underestimate what can be learned. Don't underestimate a person's knowledge or ability. Don't underestimate that you know what makes that person tick. GSDers have often been underestimated and have learned from each of those situations and used them as fuel to improve and make themselves better.

After considering all those lessons, how do we learn something from every experience? One of the things I like to do after an experience is facilitate my own debrief, a review of sorts. For example, I might ask:

- Did I accomplish what I set out to do?

- What could I have done better or worse?

- How could I have responded differently?

- Did I ask questions?

- Did I listen?

- Did I hear?

- Did my point of view come across?

- Did I listen to their point of view with patience and curiosity?

ACTIVITY

What types of questions do you ask yourself after experiencing something positive?

_____

_____

_____

_____

What types of questions do you ask yourself after experiencing something negative? Make note of the difference between the two types of questions you ask yourself. How do you feel about yourself after positive and negative experiences?

_____

_____

_____

_____

In addition to recognizing that there is a learning opportunity in every situation, life has also allowed me to develop the ability to determine whether a lesson is one that will teach future me what TO DO or what NOT TO DO. I have had lots of mentors and heroes from whom I have learned both sides of this equation. I believe we can look to those in our lives or from a distance and ask, "What can I learn from you so that I don't have to live it?"

Perhaps throughout your life, you have had relationships that were chosen for you or that you encountered that weren't always the best. Maybe they came with a lot of toxic or negative interactions. Within each of these moments, you are faced with two choices: you could be bitter or angry because you have to engage with those people, or you could choose to look at their lives or choices from a different viewpoint.

Both my parents have taught me these extremely valuable lessons, especially in our familial dynamics and interactions. My father and I didn't always have the best father-daughter relationship. It was messy. It was complicated. We certainly had some precious memories that I will treasure, but it wasn't an easy relationship. We both had to work hard to make the relationship work. At times, we took breaks from it, and that's okay. In our own ways, we were both broken people, and that didn't always bring out the best in us. However, towards the latter years of my dad's life, we were able to get really honest. In one of these moments of truth, I said to him, "I love you. I will honor you as my father because that's what our faith calls for. You will always be my dad, but there are times, in my life, when you have taught me more of what not to do than what to do."

These words, as honest as they were, were not the easiest to say, and they weren't the easiest for him to hear. However, in his last letter to me before he died, he acknowledged them. He was grateful for the reconciliation we had worked so hard for. He acknowledged that my words were true and that he was sorry he couldn't have done better. He asked that I continue to live my life and grow my family but that I not forget him; that I share stories with my kids about their Papa Teddy; and that I be sure to share not only the good lessons but also the lessons he wished he had learned earlier.

Readers have shared that they are surprised to hear of my honesty and transparency around my familial relationships. There seem to be two camps of responses. The first is they assume that I had an amazingly healthy, always positive, issueless upbringing. The second is surprise that, given how much I learned of what not to do, how I could share how those negative situations made me a better human and not a bitter one.

The GSD Factor mindset is one that suggests that we look at our experiences as glass half-full, not half-empty. Many people question how I'm so positive and how I'm always able to look at life like the glass is half-full. I think it's because my mindset is always on learning something from every experience. Even in those less-than-optimal or outright negative situations there is something to be gleaned. There is something to be stored in the playbook, to be able to recall and replay at a moment's notice.

That's why I can share the stories that I share about life, be it familial or professional, in a transparent, vulnerable, and honest way without bitterness or resentment but rather gratitude, thankfulness, and appreciation.

That moment of acknowledging that someone in your life, be it a family member, boss, or friend, is actually teaching you what not to do can be extremely impactful. That's when you have to confront the tough, unblocked, unfiltered realities of life. The fullness of those lessons makes a much greater impact on our lives than we may realize. I think, in this society, we just expect that we are going to be taught what to do, how to do it, and get all the steps to success explicitly. It's less popular to look at a situation and ask, "What did I learn *not* to do?"

My challenge to you is this: look back on some of your interactions, relationships, or connections, recent or otherwise, and ask yourself, "What did I learn? Did I learn what to do or what not to do?" Ask yourself these questions from a place of gratitude, and it will completely transform your outlook on the past and present. Learning from the past opens up opportunities for growing in your future. This newfound inquisitiveness will allow you a level of grace and forgiveness, should you want it, that will give you wings of freedom. You won't regret past decisions or mistakes because you will realize that you are still able to learn from those things, and these lessons will help you get stuff done.

ACTIVITY

Think of a person who impacts your life, positively or negatively.

_____

_____

What has that person taught you to do?

_____

_____

What has that person taught you not to do?

_____

_____

Take some time to reflect on a time someone taught you what not to do. Maybe their actions had harmful or negative effects on you. Consider what experiences that person may have had that influenced his/her actions. Can you offer compassion, empathy, or understanding to that person, despite the negative effects their actions had on you, especially if you still learned a valuable lesson in the process?

A SPACE TO DREAM BIG . . .

A SPACE TO DREAM BIG . . .

GSD FACTOR CLAN

We are meant to have a community or a team. I like to think of this community as my GSD Factor Clan. I'm drawn to the word clan due to my Celtic lineage and ancestry across Wales, Ireland, and Scotland. In early Scottish history, clans had specialties or focuses like hunting, farming, sewing, or music. Within each of those clans, there were roles and responsibilities for each family. For example, a couple of families were the educators for the children, or the tradesman for the goods that were hunted, grown, or created. Whatever their role was within their specialty, every person had a purpose. They had a contribution to make, and this was well-communicated and known within the tribal clan and community at large.

ACTIVITY

Before reading any further, make a list of who you consider to be part of your clan.

_____

_____

_____

_____

_____

_____

_____

_____

You are the leader of your own GSD Factor Clan. No ifs, ands, or buts on this one. You, and only you alone, can fulfill this role and its responsibilities. As we embark on building your GSD Factor Clan, know that communicating to your individual Clan members that you consider them to be part of your Clan is key. Additionally, it's important, especially if it's a friend or family member, to ask them if they are willing to be part of your GSD Factor Clan. You are going to reach out to them. Look to them for guidance and feedback. Identifying, naming, communicating, and getting buy-in from your GSD Factor Clan will ensure your success as you are on this GSD Factor transformation.

If you were able to name a number of people, that's great! Raised as a Liverpool Football Club fan, I heard "You'll Never Walk Alone" played and sung throughout our house and many family gatherings. The words ring so true: "Walk on, walk on. With hope in your heart. And you'll never walk alone." This journey called life was never meant for us to be alone or do it alone. As we grow up, we experience different, sometimes difficult things that may make us *feel* alone, but it is important to believe and understand that, even then, we are never alone. Even in a world where families are separated by thousands of miles and the familial generational unit is less common, we still look to our families, those to whom we've been born and those we have chosen. Iron sharpens iron. We can support one another. We know that we can learn from one another. We watch each other.

If you named one or two people, that's amazing too! Your journey so far may have looked less crowded than others, but at the end of the day, you have at least one person who has helped or is helping you along the way. Fighter pilots don't just have a co-pilot; they have a wingman. That wingman is there to maintain formation no matter if it's in front, behind, or to the side. They are constantly watching out for the main fighter pilot and running interference if necessary.

Now that you have thought about your current Clan, think about the types of roles each member plays in your life. There are a lot of different roles and responsibilities that Clan members can take. Here are different types that you can consider:

- Your Spiritual member

- Your Mental Health member

- Your Self-Care member

- Your Physical member

- Your Hero member

- Your Dreamer member

- Your Execution member

- Your Cheerleader member

You may have several people that fulfill multiple roles, but each role brings a distinct value to your life. Your GSD Factor Clan should grow and evolve with you as you are ever-growing and evolving. We humans must continue to grow, learn, be stretched, and be challenged. Your GSD Factor Clan should do the same, and if it's not, then friend, it's time to evaluate and make sure your members are meeting you where you are on your journey.

YOUR SPIRITUAL CLAN MEMBER

My spiritual side recommends having a spiritual member. Perhaps it's a priest or pastor, or if you don't have a formal faith practice, then you can still seek out spiritual guides. Being in alignment with a higher power and ensuring you are nurturing your soul are foundational cornerstones for your life.

MENTAL HEALTH CLAN MEMBER

Be sure to think about your soul, spirit, mind, and body and whether they are fully represented in your GSD Factor Clan. We have touched a little bit on soul and even spirit, but the mind is just as important. You need that mental health Clan member. It could be a therapist, school counselor, personal coach, or even all of the above.

YOUR SELF-CARE CLAN MEMBER

Similar to the mental health Clan member is the self-care Clan member who is equally as important. Think of what the flight attendants tell plane travelers as they are reciting the safety procedures. They always say, "Please put on your mask before helping others." We should think of self-care in the same way. Be sure your self-care centers around being loving, present, and extending grace and mercy to yourself first. It helps to have someone in your life who will remind you of that.

YOUR PHYSICAL CLAN MEMBER

Next, is your physical Clan member. This is a great time to share an example of Clan members who serve in more than one capacity. One of my mental health Clan members is also my physical Clan member because the practice incorporates both mental and physical exercises. Your physical member encourages you to get your body moving in some way. That could be through walking outside and embracing nature and the energy that comes from that. Your physical Clan member could also be the physical trainer who is pushing and stretching you, making sure you are the healthiest version of *you*. This member could also be a yogi who wants to focus on your breath and the cleansing and centering that breathing brings. What's your physical go to? There is scientific evidence that supports that physical exercise is beneficial to our bodies, minds, and emotions, so do not neglect this member!

YOUR HERO CLAN MEMBER

The hero Clan member is who you aspire to be like. It could be someone you know or even someone you don't know at all. It could be someone who is alive or has passed. Consider someone in your community, your parents, teachers, athletes, or artists. Whoever your hero is, they should inspire you to be the best version of yourself. They should be someone you can look to when your journey becomes difficult and you need that extra push to keep showing up.

YOUR DREAMER CLAN MEMBERS

Now let's talk about the dreamer or the visionary Clan member. If you struggle to dream or cast a vision for yourself, find that person who will be your dreamer and your visionary. We can get so caught in the daily rhythm of life that we forget to dream, forget to think about the horizon and possibilities. When we dream, it unlocks that hope of possibility. It unlocks creativity. It unlocks what *could* be. Think about someone who inspires you, maybe they are a friend or someone famous you have read about or watched, perhaps they have accomplished things that you want to accomplish. Your dreamer Clan member is the person who will get you to think and see your life in ways that you cannot or struggle to imagine.

YOUR EXECUTION CLAN MEMBERS

With any dream or vision, you also need a plan to execute. This is where your execution Clan member comes in. Just think, you know where you are today and you know where you want to go, but do you have a roadmap or plan to get there? You need the map with the milestones that need to be hit in order to achieve. This person is your execution master. They will guide you, remind you of what needs to be done to reach that dream or vision in the timeline or date you set for yourself, and assist you in completing these goals and projects. Consider your colleagues, former supervisors, coaches, or friends–whomever you call when you need to get stuff done. As with all of the GSD Factor Clan positions, this execution member will really be unique to your life and needs. Whoever it is, this person helps you get stuff done in the most literal sense.

YOUR CHEERLEADER CLAN MEMBER

Many times, people associate their encouragement or cheerleader with their execution master, but I would argue you don't necessarily want them to be the same person. Your cheerleader is the person who allows you to express your feelings, hears your cries and screams. Your cheerleader helps pick you back up, dusts you off, and reminds you of your dreams. Ideally, everybody in your Clan will be cheering you on and encouraging you in some way, but it's good to know that you have a few people that you can go to and always get support and motivation.

ACTIVITY

Now that you know the GSD Factor Clan roles, fill in the people in your life who serve as your members.

My Spiritual member is _____

My Mental Health member is _____

My Self-Care member is _____

My Physical member is _____

My Hero member is _____

My Dreamer member is _____

My Execution member is _____

My Cheerleader member is _____

This GSD Factor Clan is important because it's imperative to get the input of others. Living The GSD Factor Life means being fully aware that you do not know everything, nor are you the best at everything. The healthy GSDer knows that and is not hesitant to tap their Clan members on the shoulder for help when necessary.

Remember that some of your GSD Factor Clan members may serve in a couple of member roles. For example, your self-care member might also be your physical member, or your dreamer is also your cheerleader. That's fine. This is your GSD Factor Clan. You get to build and pull together those clan members for you. And do not forget that what your GSD Factor Clan looks like today may not be the GSD Factor Clan you need tomorrow. As you continue to grow in your GSD Factor transformation, so will your Clan. Take the time to re-evaluate your Clan on a regular cadence and make sure they are who you need in this season.

A SPACE TO DREAM BIG . . .

A SPACE TO DREAM BIG . . .

A SPACE TO DREAM BIG . . .

GSD FACTOR INSIDERS BOARD

Most entities in the corporate world, be they businesses, universities, non-profit organizations, etc. have a board of directors. A board of directors is the governing body of a company. The purpose of these boards is to oversee activities, provide guidance, and be advocates for the organization they are representing. Members can be elected, selected, or hired, but obtaining and maintaining a seat on a board is usually a sign that one's opinion and expertise are valuable and respected. Within the sports world, there is a term for a person in media who has connections, making them privy to information unavailable to others, literally the insider scoop of what is going on in that club or team.

We talked about our GSD Factor Clan and how important it is to have those people close to us and in place, but I also want to float this idea past you: If you were to assemble your own "GSD Factor Insiders Board?" What type of people would you pick? What kinds of things would you run past them?

Your GSD Factor Insiders Board is composed of a different group of people than your GSD Factor Clan. Your Insiders Board is made up of individuals who won't let you get away with anything. They are the people who challenge you professionally, first, then personally, which is the opposite of your clan. Your GSD Factor Clan makes sure that you, as a person, are developing, being nurtured, and holding space for the right things, be they spiritual, physical, mental, etc. Your GSD Factor Insiders Board will challenge your business decisions and strategies, hold you accountable, and do anything to ensure your success professionally.

Similar to my GSD Factor Clan, I have listed the positions that make up my Insiders Board. Some of them serve the same purpose as the Clan positions, but the focus is professional rather than personal. The roles are:

- Administrator member
- Tech and Data member
- Visionary member
- Execution member

YOUR ADMINISTRATOR BOARD MEMBER

The first Insiders Board member we'll explore is your administrator. The administrator is detail-oriented, dotting the *i*'s and crossing those *t*'s to make sure things are as they should be. You could have multiple members of this type with specialty focuses such as legal, financial, etc. In some cases, your administrator board member and execution board member are one in the same, but this person is just making sure that whatever you are doing is being done with organization, flawless execution, and professionalism, all while remaining financially and legally friendly. Sometimes, this member may be you.

YOUR TECH & DATA BOARD MEMBER

The next member category is the tech and data board member. They will help you stay up to date on the latest technology platforms to keep engagement up or help you to understand what science and data are being researched and published. I have a few of these members. They are all people that I have worked with at other companies whose work ethic and expertise impressed me so much that I asked them to join me as advisors for my businesses. They accepted and are integral parts of my team. Depending on you and your Insiders Board, you may decide you need a separate technology and separate data board member, and that is ok. Out of all the members, this one could easily be a vendor that you engage with to handle all this. Whatever it is, technology and data are significantly changing each and every day. Your profession, industry, and company will help you determine the level of tech and data GSD Factor Insiders Board members you need.

YOUR VISIONARY & EXECUTION BOARD MEMBERS

These last two members–your visionary and execution member–serve in the same capacity as the Clan members of the same name. The visionary member will help you dream big in your professional life and push you to make those dreams a reality. Because I have so many big dreams and visions for my companies, I have a few different execution members, depending on the organizations' needs. These members keep me on track and help me actually carry out the plans and visions. As with the rest of your Insiders Board, your execution members are customizable and dependent upon your needs and your industry. Members will change as you grow and change professionally, so make sure you are constantly aware of what you need and how your execution members can help.

ACTIVITY

Now that you know the GSD Factor Insiders Board roles, fill in the people in your life who serve as your members.

My Administrator member is _____

My Tech and Data member is _____

My Visionary member is _____

My Execution member is_____

ACTIVITY

Step 1: Use the chart below to list all your strengths and weaknesses.

Step 2: Next to your strengths, fill in the name of someone you know who excels in this area as well.

Step 3: Next to your weaknesses, fill in the name of someone you know who excels in this area.

Now, consider this: Could any of those people be members of your GSD Factor Clan or Insiders Board?

Maybe those people are already unofficially serving in one of those roles in your life. Whether they are or not, consider having a conversation with them explaining that you'd like to lean on them for support in that area

STRENGTH	NAME	CLAN OR INSIDERS BOARD	WEAKNESS	NAME	CLAN OR INSIDERS BOARD

A SPACE TO DREAM BIG . . .

A SPACE TO DREAM BIG . . .

HOLD WITH OPEN HANDS

Life is funny. One day, everything is going great. You feel like you're on top of the world, and the next day or the next moment, something can happen to change all of that. Suddenly, you find yourself in a season of darkness and despair. And even in some cases, you can feel both in back-to-back moments. I know both of these seasons so well, and experiencing those great highs and crushing lows taught me the important lesson of holding onto things with open hands. What do I mean by that? Holding onto things with open hands means understanding and accepting that nothing is promised to any of us. While it is normal and human to find comfort in stability and consistency, it is also important to be flexible and open to the times when things are uncertain or aren't going according to your plans.

Concerning this GSD Factor Life, I must warn you that if we hold on too tightly to things or people, we may be limiting our growth potential. One popular saying that I hear often is, "If one door closes, a window will open." It takes faith to remember that in the moment. When those doors close, it is time to channel the GSD Factor attribute that reminds us to ask ourselves what we can learn from these situations and how they can shape and mold us. That's when we need to decide if the glass is half full or not.

In a recent coaching call, my client was in the midst of a professional transformation. She had outlined what she wanted in her next role, including responsibilities, what brought her joy and meaning in her work, what industry she wanted to shift into, and what kind of organization she wanted to be aligned with. She had many successful interviews with numerous organizations across varying industries, but the job that she really wanted was stalling. During this stall, she received a job offer for something she had done before and had been successful at, but it wasn't challenging. She would have seen it as a step backward, not forward. Some gave her the advice that she should be grateful for a job in this economy. They advised that she just take the offer and pivot into something later. I simply asked questions. What was her gut saying? What was her heart saying? Immediately, she articulated what she truly wanted. She already knew she needed to let that job offer go because it was the safe and complacent choice. She knew if she didn't let it go, something better couldn't come into being. I encouraged her to follow her intuition; gratefully decline the offer; but also push the other company to a faster decision. The job she wanted did come through with a little nudging, but we discussed that even if it hadn't, she was glad she challenged herself to wait for the right opportunity to open up. This is what it means to hold both jobs with open hands.

I've lived through enough experiences to know when my hands are holding onto something too tightly. In those moments, I gently remind myself to take a deep breath and open them. I can recall one particular example of having to hold things with open hands in my professional life.

I had a client that was excited for me to come GSD for a long-term project. However, pretty quickly into the engagement, things were not working out as originally expected, and I found myself in a toxic environment and situation. Now, I had been in this type of situation before, but this time was different. You see, it was the same year that I was publishing my first book. Throughout the two years of writing, rewriting, and rewriting some more I had put tangible words and thoughts to my experiences. I had created questions and checkpoints for readers to check in with themselves to understand what they were experiencing. I used those questions for myself, and how I responded to this toxic situation was different. I did not allow it to change me. I did not allow it to stop me from using my voice or living out my true, authentic self. In fact, I was confident enough to suggest that the contract end earlier than originally agreed.

I let go of that toxic client right as my tiny humans were embarking on their summer schedules. Because I let go at the right time, I was able to be present with them during a season that had historically been one of my busiest. That summer, they gave me the nickname "Muber" or Momma Uber because I was the one running them around from thing to thing. We mini-vacationed multiple times to water parks, theme parks, and my most favorite, the Space and Rocket Center in Huntsville, Alabama. I was able to walk the museum and share how their great-grandfather was part of the race to the moon.

It didn't really hit me how I was being present with them that summer and being able to do so much with them because I had let go of that toxic client until my daughter was writing her first essay for school where she had to write about her summer. She gave a glowing review of all that we did but said her most favorite thing was the amount of time she was able to spend with me. By living those months with open hands, out outflowed the bad and inflowed the good and solidified core memories with my tiny humans.

Hold your Clan, Insiders Board, companies, opportunities, and employees with open hands. Open hands means allowing the right things to flow in and the wrong things to flow out. Letting go of the wrong, negative, or toxic elements always leads to greater growth, opportunity, beauty, and ultimately, success that you never dreamed possible. Basically, embrace where you are, but don't be so set and firm in those situations that you get all bent out of shape when different opportunities, challenges, or unexpected changes occur. Rather, when life does start to throw curve balls, take that time to remember the GSD Factor attributes and be inquisitive. Ask yourself, "Why might this be happening? What can I learn from this? How can I grow from this? Is my current opportunity still serving me, or is it time to move on?" Those questions will help you release the hold you had on your security or your plans, all while you build character and increase in wisdom from the new challenges set before you.

A SPACE TO DREAM BIG . . .

A SPACE TO DREAM BIG . . .

HOW TO BE INQUISITIVE

The key to being inquisitive is understanding that we are always learning, which we can often do through our relationships with others. As lifelong learners, it is imperative to be surrounded by the right people. Non-judgemental accountability makes everyone better. It is also important to note that the people we surround ourselves with may change as we grow and evolve as humans and that this is okay.

As you build your GDS Factor Clan and GSD Factor Insiders Boards, you may choose people who already know you because you know they have your best interests at heart. However, you may decide that you want your GSD Factor Insiders Board to come from a new network of people, for a fresh perspective and new insights, and are considering joining outside groups to build up your Insiders Board. Either path can be right for you; just remember to exercise discernment. Stay inquisitive and ask questions. I get lots of questions from my clients and network about this growing demand and offering of memberships, clubs, groups, or collectives. While I believe that each of these has good intentions and meaningful outputs, I think that some are taking advantage of individuals, especially under-represented or under-voiced groups that are so hungry to be part of something, eager for deeper connections and a sense of belonging, be it in person or virtually. Many are extremely active and supportive of all members, but many have also veered into extremely pricey admissions, expensive add-ons in order to participate, and extensive applications and vetting processes.

Let me be clear. Everyone should be paid their worth and for their time, knowledge, and talents. And I don't disagree that there should be some kind of vetting process to determine if that person is the best fit. What concerns me are those who use cost or the application process to be selective to the privileged; those who are not necessarily making sure that there is diversity and inclusion. Some even go as far as encouraging financially unsound choices in order to pay the entrance fee. Trust your gut and just know that you don't have to spend a lot of money, if any, or put yourself in a bind to find people who want to support you.

When you are looking at building either your Clan or Insiders Board, consider those that are free first and have your best intentions at heart. Once you are in a stable financial place, then pay away, but please never take on unnecessary financial stress to be part of something. If you do decide to be part of something, have a regular cadence to check in with yourself about whether it continues serving you. And include your existing Clan or Insiders Board to ensure that the ROI or return on investment is there for you, your team, and your organization.

Being inquisitive gives you the humble awareness that you are not the smartest person in the room, but the knowledge to know how to mobilize the right team of people to ensure that you are open to the fullness of life. Be curious and ask questions. Look at life with a glass half-full approach, and search for lessons in what to do and what not to do.

A Mantra for Being Inquisitive

I am curious.

I am inquisitive.

I watch.

I listen.

I learn from everything.

I learn from everyone.

I am smart.

I am humble.

I am happy.

Positive energy surrounds me.

I am never alone.

I am always learning.

I will always have all that I need.

A SPACE TO DREAM BIG . . .

ATTRIBUTE THREE

BE **IMAGINATIVE**

Being imaginative means dreaming big.
It means saying yes to the seemingly impossible and
pushing yourself beyond even your own imagination.

"The biggest adventure you can ever take is to live the life of your dreams."

– OPRAH

ACTIVITY

If there were no obstacles in your way, who would you be? What job or role would you do? Where would you live?

_____

_____

_____

_____

_____

_____

_____

_____

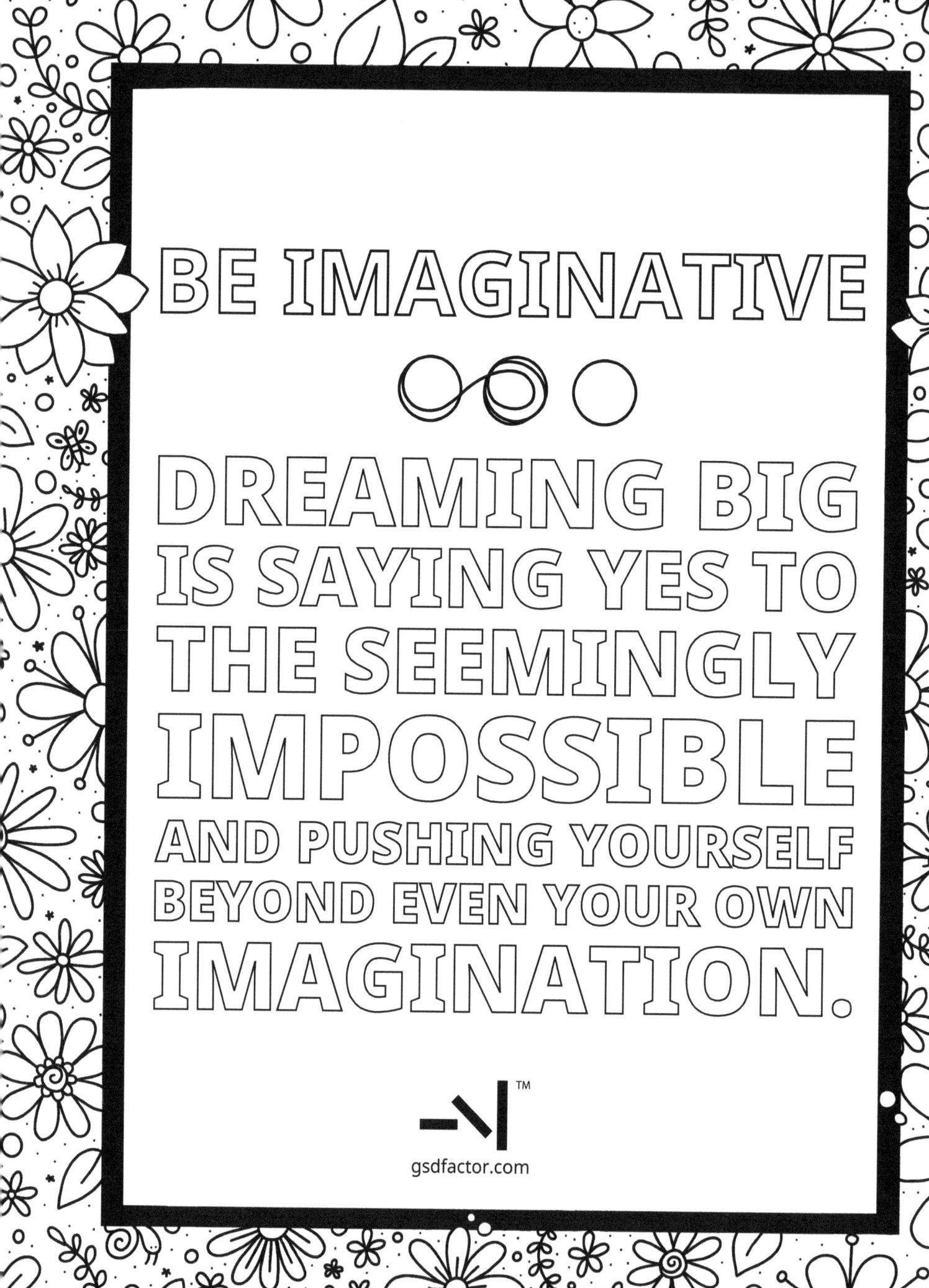

BE IMAGINATIVE

DREAMING BIG IS SAYING YES TO THE SEEMINGLY IMPOSSIBLE AND PUSHING YOURSELF BEYOND EVEN YOUR OWN IMAGINATION.

gsdfactor.com

DREAM BIG

There are not many conversations where I don't reference the phrase, "dream big" in some capacity. Imagination and dreams go hand-in-hand. For the first sixteen years of my life, my dream was dancing, but after facing sickness and injury, I realized that dreams could change. The injuries I incurred necessitated the change, but the experience shed light on dreams that were always there—dreams of entrepreneurship, mentoring, and organizational leadership. I had been operating in those dreams all my life, but because dance was my number-one priority, those other dreams just moved to the back burner. The third GSD Factor attribute—being imaginative—is all about keeping that dream-big muscle active and recognizing all the possibilities of your back-burner dreams.

As someone who is highly organized, follows rules when appropriate, and has everything planned out, my ability to dream had to evolve. My difficulty came in allowing myself to dream freely, to resist the urge to be practical and logistical, and to just let my imagination run wild. Sometimes, I have to force myself to dream, but thankfully, I have people who remind me to do so. I'm now operating fully in entrepreneurship and mentorship, so my dreams look different. They still involve a great deal of imagination, but now my dreams are all about being open to the opportunities that become available to me, recognizing the right opportunities as they arise, and knowing how to be in the moment.

Perhaps that's why I've gotten good at helping people dream big for themselves and their organizations. There are times or situations in people's lives when dreaming big is necessary. Perhaps they were laid off or there was a merger or acquisition where jobs were redundant. Maybe university is coming to an end and they need help figuring out the next step. Or maybe they are shifting from one career into another but aren't sure what that other is just yet.

One particular client of mine was retiring from a twenty-year career serving in our armed forces and was ready for the next chapter. As a family with many military ties, I've seen this story time and time again. The military does a solid job of identifying a person's strengths and skills, applying them where needed, and moving them up the ranks and through various roles and responsibilities while also providing support in the areas of housing, transportation, health services, etc. It's a well-oiled machine of work-life-family integration running optimally and efficiently. However, translating that professional work into the civilian sector can be more of a challenge. Many people struggle even more with how to transition their experience across the rest of their life; both to achieve their long-term goals and for their civilian daily life.

With this client, I conducted what I like to call Dream Big sessions, where we were able to break down the client's skills, likes and dislikes, and successes and failures to start formulating what a job for them would look like in the corporate world. Anytime there is a transition like this, it's important to pause, celebrate what you have accomplished, and conduct self-awareness retrospectives so that you can give space to not only this transition but ultimately give space to this next dream and chapter in your life.

When I think about the evolution of my dreams, I can see now that what I saw as a hindrance to my dreams—the way I leaned toward practicality and logic—could actually be an asset, as long as there is a balance between logic and imagination. A major part of being imaginative and dreaming big is to figure out how to transform those dreams into reality. The best way to do that is just to allow yourself to dream. Let your imagination roam freely, but then access your practical mind and the ways to make the impossible happen.

I had a recent conversation with another client who shared that her organization had no problem with dreaming big, but their Achilles heel was they didn't execute those dream bigs. They did not get stuff done. This repeated pattern it actually started to stunt the dreaming big muscle within the organization because there wasn't trust that it was worth dreaming big and sharing because nothing would come of it.

In season one of *Ted Lasso*, as Ted is trying to be influential with his new team, he creates a suggestions box and asks all parties to provide their thoughts, feedback, ideas, and ultimately their dream bigs. The one actionable thing in all the suggestions was increasing the water pressure in the showers. Now, for the person suggesting it, it could have been seen as a minor thing or been seen as a dream big, but no matter the intent, this was someone's idea, and Ted knew he had to execute and turn that dream into a reality. Why? Because we are human, and we respond well to seeing things come to fruition, especially when they were our idea, or we used our voice to bring awareness to it. We get excited even at the smallest of things. Often, we get more excited when some of those smallest things create an impact beyond ourselves but on others, too. Sometimes, when organizations need to dream big, they need to execute the low-hanging fruit because it stunts the growth of the bigger ideas and dreams.

How do you access your practical mind to make the impossible happen? That's where you have to do a little work. Dreaming big is great, but until you put a plan together, it's just a dream. You might have to look for people who have done similar things. Do some research. Your dream may seem impossible now, but you'd be surprised how much more attainable it becomes once you start discovering other people who have achieved similar feats. Seeing these other successes and even some failures can be just the motivation and inspiration you need to make your dreams happen. It's going to take some effort, but that's how we get stuff done.

With dreaming big, you may, at times, experience failing big. Sometimes, we must fail in order to see how dream bigs become reality. Yes, we use our imaginations and do our best to plan and execute those plans in hopes of the best possible outcome, but dreaming big necessitates the awareness that every plan will not be successful on the first attempt. This is part of the beauty of the whole process. When you dream big, you give yourself permission to make mistakes. But unfortunately, most people and companies are not willing to do it. It's a risky process that takes tenacity, endurance, and stamina to be successful. It is a risk, and it's not easy.

In the process of completing a project, I actually want my teams to try and fail fast and try again. But the ultimate goal, the ultimate objective, and that ultimate date—those items are what can't fail. I encourage my teams to see the process of executing the dream as a series of attempts at success. The project or vision didn't happen the way we envisioned on the first attempt. Okay, so we accept that, correct the errors, and try again. That's how we reach success.

Why do I want my teams to fail fast and try again? It's simple. *We learn quickly.* It makes us agile. It teaches us to adapt and pivot. It causes us to realize what works and what doesn't work quickly. And ultimately, it makes us better at what we do today and into the future.

Part of this mindshift is being ok with good enough. It would seem that a perspective like this would actually be counterintuitive to the idea of dreaming big, but sometimes it is more productive to accept the idea of good enough. Many experiences have reminded me that sometimes we have to focus on progress and not perfection. It's worth repeating: we have to *focus on progress and not perfection* to achieve our dream bigs.

ACTIVITY

Grab three note cards or sticky notes, and write down one dream big or ambition on each note card/sticky note. If you don't have them on hand, use these as placeholders until you acquire some.

Don't think about how big or impossible the dream seems. Just write it down and place them around your room, office, or other personal space that you see every day. Look over them. Read them out loud. Dream about them. You are manifesting them, which means you are calling them to happen.

A SPACE TO DREAM BIG . . .

NEVER BE SATISFIED

My grandfather, General Joseph S. Bleymaier, or Papa Joe as we called him, was a major general in the United States Air Force who fought in World War II and led Air Force support efforts for NASA in the race to the moon and the Titan rocket program. He would later become known as the "Father of the Titan III Missile" and be awarded some of our country's highest honors due to his contributions to air research and development. He was brilliant, a literal rocket scientist. Because of my grandfather's history with NASA and the Space Program, I've always been fascinated and inspired by the Space Race of the sixties.

There was a speech on May 25, 1961, in which President John F. Kennedy delivered a special message to Congress on Urgent National Needs. This address is considered to be the first moon speech, in which he said, "First, I believe that this nation should commit itself to achieving the goal, before this decade is out, of landing a man on the moon and returning him safely to the earth." He later reiterated, "I believe we should go to the moon." This speech really spearheaded the support, commitment, and resources needed from the government and the nation. President Kennedy's words are at the crux of the GSD Factor attribute of being imaginative, and they coincide with the sub attribute—never be satisfied.

This wasn't a small project. It was putting a man on the moon and returning him back to Earth safely, which was a feat no one had done, and especially not with a program that was behind the technological curve. For example, in order to complete interstellar orbits, one of the first things we needed was satellites, and the first working satellite, Sputnik, was not created by the U.S., but by the Soviet Union. We've talked about being imaginative as it relates to dreaming big, and never being satisfied is the next step to maximizing your imagination's potential. The United States' dedication to winning the Space Race is a great example of this type of ideology because of all the seemingly insurmountable odds that our space program was facing at the time. Many said it couldn't be done. At the time, our space program was behind, very behind. The money wasn't there. The infrastructure wasn't there. We didn't have the right technology.

My grandfather was responsible for the Atlas booster that, in February of 1962, would put the first American in Earth's orbit. That astronaut was John Glenn in Friendship 7, and he would end up flying around Earth three times during that mission.

The mission and success of Friendship 7 were dramatized for the big screen in the 2017 movie *Hidden Figures,* which follows the story of three African-American female mathematicians, Katherine Goble Johnson, Dorothy Vaughan, and Mary Jackson. All of these trailblazing women embodied the GSD Factor attribute of being imaginative and are beautiful examples and inspirations to us all.

I want to focus on Dorothy Vaughan, for a moment, who was not only a human computer but the first African-American woman to be promoted to supervising a group of human computers. Even while being treated unfairly for her work and contributions, Dorothy wanted to be sure that she was always dreaming big, never being satisfied, and staying current with all of the latest technology. During the early 1960s, not only were we trying to go to the moon, but we were also introducing computers into our professional careers and workplaces. Dorothy witnessed the IBM 790 Data Processing System (DPS) being installed at NASA and knew that the goal would be to replace her and her fellow human computers. She decided at that moment to take it upon herself to ensure that she learned and adapted to this technology.

Dorthy taught herself and her team the Fortran programming language that allowed them to program and run the IBM 790 DPS. When these computers came out, people thought that they would immediately replace humans; they hadn't yet understood that the computers needed to be programmed and run by humans. The technology certainly provided automation and time savings, but human minds were still needed to ensure this new and innovative technology worked as it should. Dorothy was never satisfied in that she didn't allow technology to replace her but made sure that technology enhanced her abilities and the abilities of her team.

With the successful mission of Friendship 7 came a shift in momentum for Americans. Now that the tide had turned in our favor with the success of being the first to send a crew into space to orbit the moon, we couldn't stop there. We weren't satisfied with just orbiting the moon. As the country prepared for the next moon race phase, President John F. Kennedy addressed the nation in September 1962. He famously said, "We choose to go to the Moon in this decade and do the other things, not because they are easy, but because they are hard....But if I were to say, my fellow citizens, that we shall send to the moon... and do all this, and do it right, and do it first before this decade is out—then we must be bold."

Talk about pressure! Think of how daunting a task that already was, but adding a timeline of fewer than eight years made it especially impossible. Still, with the backing of our president, our country, and our citizens, we said yes. We embodied boldness. We innovated. We DREAMED BIG. In July of 1969, with less than six months left in the decade, we did it. That moment is memorialized by Neil Armstrong's famous quote, "That's one small step for a man, one giant leap for mankind."

If you're wondering why the space program is near and dear to my heart, it's because there are lots of connections between the moon landing and my career in the technology industry and The GSD Factor. You could say it runs in my blood. The GSD Factor didn't start with me; it flows through my DNA, and it came from my grandfather. It was his contribution to and involvement with the space program that makes it a little more special to me. He was a part of the people who weren't satisfied with being second best. My grandfather said yes to the president. He said yes to his country by leading some of these special projects during this pivotal time in our country's technological history. He dreamed big. Today, he has an award in the Smithsonian, and his many decorations include the Legion of Merit and the Air Medal with oak leaf cluster.

In 2017, he was added to the General Schriever Wall of Honor at the Space & Missile Systems Center at Los Angeles Air Force Base, California. This memorial was constructed as a way to honor and recognize some of the earliest pioneers in space who have made tremendous contributions to our community, nation, and humanity. Each year, a new class of names is added to the Schriever Wall of Honor. After my dad's death, my sister and I had the honor of standing in for him and being there for the revealing of our grandfather's name on that wall. I was even more honored to have my own daughter, his great-granddaughter, there as well. Sitting there surrounded by my aunt and uncles, my fellow Bleymaiers, hearing the accomplishments and achievements of Papa Joe Bleymaier, I felt a great sense of pride, gratitude, and a weight of responsibility as if he was passing the torch of innovation on to my sister and me. It was the torch of dreaming big, the reminder to never say never, challenging the status quo and asking "Why not?" It was the torch of choosing possible instead of impossible. He passed this ideology on to his five children and sixteen grandchildren, who will continue to pass it on for generations to come.

ACTIVITY

Name someone who dreamed beyond what had already been done to achieve something new that you admire. Why have you chosen this person?

_____

_____

_____

_____

_____

The drive of never being satisfied and never settling embodied my grandfather's life and mission, and he passed this to me as one of the key attributes of The GSD Factor Life. I've also faced challenges in my professional career that were similar to those that my grandfather had to face during the space race. One of those times came in March 2020, right as the United States implemented the first mandatory shutdown of the country. The COVID-19 pandemic was probably one of the most uncertain health crises of our lifetime, and because I had just been hired as the new head of technology for an insurance company, my team and I were now being asked to make drastic technological changes in the face of uncertainty and navigating how we would be able to interact with our customers. The short version of our task was that we needed to rebuild, rethink, and re-engineer what technology would look like to serve the insurance community in the midst of a pandemic. Oh, yeah, and we had to do it in six months!

For the next several months, my team and I worked hundred-hour work weeks to build technology that would allow us to complete insurance quotes for clients and go through the enrollment process electronically, which had historically been done in person. The technology was so innovative and game-changing that we started garnering the attention of our competitors, government agencies, and eventually buyers. Our technology stack was the catalyst that led to the company's acquisition in December of that same year. For me, that whole experience further solidified the never-be-satisfied genes I inherited from my grandfather.

Even now, the technology space is being challenged with another innovation of Artificial Intelligence (AI). AI is here to stay, and we are still learning each and every day its benefits and its downfalls. We are also learning where this automation is best applied and, more importantly, where not to apply it. Many think AI will replace humans, but I would challenge that AI's place is not to replace but rather augment, enhance, and provide humans with automation opportunities where it makes sense, especially as we are trying to get more stuff done. As exciting as new technology is, including AI, we must not forget when to use humans, when to use technology, and when both can co-exist and collaborate. This is why, in October of 2023, my companies announced our Declaration of Authenticity. I have always created human-generated content, and my team and I are committed to continually producing, writing, and editing human-created content across all of our services and offerings.

Part of dreaming big and never being satisfied is knowing where to draw that integrity and authenticity line and take that stand, even when it's not the popular thing to do, but it is the right thing to do. I know that I come from ancestors on both sides of my family who embraced and amplified innovation, drive, dreaming big, and never being satisfied, but I believe that this lives within each of us. Whether your ancestral history has examples of this for you to follow or not, you are responsible for your history, *your story*, the story that your lineage will speak about. Ask yourself, "What should I never be satisfied about?" Whatever it is, try saying yes, because in the words of famed American author and activist Glennon Doyle, "We can do hard things."

So don't avoid those difficulties or challenges. Tackle them head-on with your imagination and that spirit of never being satisfied. Who knows? You may surprise yourself and impact history just like my grandfather and the ingenious men and women he worked with during the Space Race.

ACTIVITY

Answer the following questions about yourself:

What situation do you find yourself in that you are not satisfied with?

_____

_____

_____

_____

Is there something you have observed in your community that stirs an excitement that makes you want to take action?

_____

_____

_____

_____

A SPACE TO DREAM BIG . . .

PROBLEMS LEAD TO SOLUTIONS

Everyone has problems. People have problems getting along with co-workers, problems saving money, problems maintaining healthy lifestyles. The list goes on.

ACTIVITY

Give yourself ten seconds and name three problems (big or small) that you have.

_____

_____

_____

_____

_____

_____

Everyone also *sees* problems. These are problems that are noticeable to everyone but can't necessarily be changed on an individual level. For example, we see problems with the environment, problems with the education system, problems in politics, and even problems we see with our friends, family members, or co-workers.

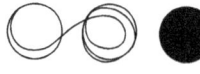

ACTIVITY

Give yourself ten seconds and name three problems that you've seen but can't change on your own.

_____

_____

_____

_____

_____

_____

_____

_____

Now, problems are unavoidable. Whether at home, at work, among family, or among friends, we all face them. I believe, though, that the way we approach problems separates us into two types of people: problem-pointers and problem-solvers.

There is a great book by Kirk A. Weisler called, *The Dog Poop Initiative*, which provides a great lesson into problem-pointers and problem-solvers. The book's purpose is to teach readers how to be proactive citizens who make efforts to better every environment they are in, even when they don't necessarily have to.

Essentially, in *The Dog Poop Initiative*, a dog takes a dump out on a soccer pitch. We won't address the fact that the owner didn't pick it up in the first place, but dog owners, you know who you are; do better. Over the course of a day, there are multiple soccer matches where parents, coaches, referees, and even kids are problem-pointers and even great problem-communicators to anyone that was coming to the pitch. The book goes on about how the pointers consistently and vehemently pointed at the poop. The communicators made sure to warn other people to avoid the poop. Some even complained about the poop. They changed where they played. They changed how they played, but no one tried to solve the problem. The author goes on to say that about two hundred and twenty people avoided the poop that day, and, in the end, only two actually took action to scoop the poop. That's not even one percent. Seriously?! That's art imitating life, though.

Think about how many times a day you hear someone complain about a problem, and compare that with how many times you actually see or hear about people who take the initiative to fix a problem that is staring right at them. The time and resources spent by the rest of the population pointing it out, complaining, and over-communicating is staggering. What if, as a population and a world, we just moved that needle just a little, even to a full one percent? How different would our world look? How different would companies run?

Being a problem-solver and not a problem-pointer is one of the main fundamentals of living The GSD Factor Life. If you find yourself on the solving side of that categorization, then you're probably a person who, as we know I like to say, gets stuff done. Don't get too excited yet, because being that type of person comes with its own set of risks. If you're a natural-born GSDer, then you don't have a problem finding and implementing solutions to problems. You know how to use your imagination to dream big, and when it comes to problem-solving, you understand how important it is to never be satisfied.

However, the real discipline for people who are born with the gift of problem-solving and GSDing comes when it's time to determine what *kind* of solution to use. I'm talking about the MVP here. No, that's not the *most valuable player*. It's the *minimum viable product*. In the business world, it has become known as the solution you can come up with that works and creates time for you to try, fail fast, and try again as you prepare for a permanent solution. Finding and applying the interim solution rather than immediately beginning work on the long-term solution is a skill that will serve problem-solvers well because it allows you the time to rest and avoid the stress of always diving head-first into long-term solutions. Now, all hope is not lost if you find yourself on the opposite side of the problem-solver/problem-pointer coin. If you're not one of those people who immediately see solutions, or perhaps you are a problem-pointer, it's okay. We are all works in progress, and you, too, can develop those skills and eventually become a master solutionist.

My high school instructor never gave out tests; he gave "opportunities." What if we thought about problems in the same way? If you think about it, you probably have "opportunities" every day—moments or challenges that, with the right perspective shift, are chances for problem-solving or growth. I have them all the time. Once you realize you have an opportunity, ask yourself if you have a solution. Am I saying that you cannot express frustrations or difficulties? No, you most certainly have a right to your frustrations, and it's healthy for you to express them. However, there is a time and a place for everything, so I do suggest that if you need to vent about something, do it in the appropriate setting, to the appropriate people, and in the appropriate manner. Otherwise, you run the risk of being perceived as a complainer.

If you're good at identifying problems or opportunities, how do you then turn towards becoming a problem solver? To be effective problem solvers, our mindset and state of being need to be unified and focused on peace. Anxiety is often our first response to problems or conflicts. Oftentimes, anxiety coupled with fear can block our brains from solutioning and finding the answers; this amplifies the fear, causing us to be insecure. We don't want to give power or add fuel to the problem, we want to work the problem. In my experience, I've learned that solutions and answers arise organically from an aligned, peaceful state of mind.

For example, have you ever been in a stressful situation, and you couldn't think straight? I've experienced this kind of stress a few times, but it was particularly recognizable as we got closer to the deadlines of a number of major projects. I was experiencing solution fatigue, which is exactly what it sounds like. My brain was tired of solving problems, so it would become increasingly more difficult for me to do so. When those times came, I didn't try to push through the fatigue. I would stop working and go for a walk or spend time with my family. Sometimes, the most practical solution would be to go take a quick power nap. I love power naps! Those power naps work wonders for my weary brain, and when I wake up, I'm refreshed and ready to get stuff done.

Why is this? For the same reason you need to shut down or restart your phone or computer sometimes, your brain needs to reboot; it needs a rest. When you wake up, you are more likely to be in a peaceful state, and suddenly, ideas start flowing. My recommendation is having something by your bed on which you can capture ideas because as you are sleeping, the brain is recharging. You may wake up with a brilliant idea that you need to record before getting back to sleep. You never know. Finding a state of rest and peace is about groundedness. It's about finding a center.

Each person finds their center in their own way, but you have to come up with a wellness plan and strategy for yourself to be able to get back to your center. If finding that peaceful state of mind is a struggle, I recommend some breathing exercises, meditations, or visualizations to aid you in that process. I've often heard that peace is a state of rest and calmness in the soul.

ACTIVITY

Think of at least three of your most recently faced problems or challenges. Do you notice any themes or similarities in the nature or scope of the challenges? Now think of the ways in which you addressed those problems. Did you allow yourself time to rest and reflect before tackling solutions? Explain.

Once you've found a peaceful mindset, presenting a problem with a solution can become much easier and more systematic. Before you can actually present a solution to a problem, it would be helpful to first identify the size and scope of the problem. To do this effectively, we need more information. We get more information by, first and foremost, listening.

One of the great attributes of a leader is their ability and willingness to listen. Sometimes, we problem-solvers are so ready to jump into action that we don't listen and miss important pieces of information. If you can't tell, I'm a problem-solver, and there are many times when I have to remind myself to stop and listen. I exercise this skill on a daily basis with my team and clients. On a personal level, my husband and I have a phrase that we use when we are sharing problems that are going on. We say, "I need you to listen," or "I need you to help me solve this." This came after a few times of us sharing with one another in hopes that the other would just listen, but instead, we jumped to solutioning. This usually caused us to miss the entire point and even propose the wrong solution because we didn't take the time to listen to the problem in its entirety.

Once you have a basic understanding of the problem, the second step is to focus on not being afraid to ask some clarifying questions. Depending on the temperature of the situation, you can ask, "May I ask some clarifying questions? It will help me navigate as I prepare a solution." If the moment is not right, revert back to listening and come back to that person at a later time to gain the clarity you need. Now that we have our problem and are gaining clarity through questions, we can continue to figure out how big our problem is, which will help make our solution more effective.

My daughter gave me a great example of this one day with some homework from her life skills class. Her school counselor used weather as the analogy for assessing problems and how to approach them. The scale she used is brilliant, and I've adapted the same ideologies to the business world.

- Windy = tiny problem, no biggie – Handle on your own.

- Rainy = small problem – Engage with a friend or colleague to solve.

- Stormy = medium problem – Engage with multiple people to solve.

- Tornado = big problem – Get help from a trusted friend or colleague to solve.

I think we can all agree that problems and challenges are an inevitable, unavoidable part of life. It would be great if more people took the initiative to be problem-solvers rather than just problem-pointers, but that's not reality. Actually, being a problem-pointer, in itself, isn't bad. There's value in being able to identify problems. However, if you're ever going to get stuff done, you've got to be able to do more than point out the problems. Furthermore, becoming the person who can effectively assess and solve problems requires you to be imaginative and open to a myriad of solutions. This is an invaluable skill and one that you will find to be helpful on your GSD Factor journey. This concept is like the culmination of dreaming big and never being satisfied. If you do those things, then you will find that solutions come much more freely than if not.

ACTIVITY

Identify a problem or opportunity in your life for which you can take the initiative to implement a solution or improvement. Write those possible solutions down, and share them with a trusted friend, mentor, or colleague. After sharing, consider implementing those possible solutions. Record your results.

ACTION PLAN

HOW TO BE IMAGINATIVE

What does it look like to be imaginative in everyday life? It's a combination of all three sub-attributes: dreaming big, never being satisfied with the status quo, and using your imagination to develop and implement solutions. People who think like this are constantly looking for ways to improve. There is no problem that doesn't have a solution. Even when we don't know of a perfect solution, the goal of the imaginative GSDer is to work the problem. You may not find the right solution immediately, but imaginative thinking can transform you into a problem-solver who isn't afraid to try, fail quickly, and try again.

Though the solutions may be born of imagination and creativity, the thought process for finding the solution can easily be broken down into a few actionable steps:

1. Center yourself so you can open up to those big dreams and solutions. There are several practices that can be helpful for centering. Some people journal, color, exercise, create art, garden, etc. You can do whatever is necessary to get you to a place of peace and stability.

2. Ask questions. This is a part of never being satisfied. When it comes to dreams and ambitions, it pays to be inquisitive, curious, and constantly in search of knowledge. Ask yourself, how can I be better? Push for the next job, that next goal, strive for the academic level or promotion. Your ability to improve will directly affect your level of success. You cannot get better if you are not constantly looking for ways to *be* better.

3. Initiate. Remember *The Dog Poop Initiative*. It is one thing to dream big and ponder all the possibilities for solutions and improvements, but the real challenge is taking the initiative to put all of these thoughts and considerations into practice. Will you be a problem-pointer or problem-solver?

As you make these steps of centering yourself to dream big and asking questions and initiating, you will become more comfortable with being imaginative, and soon, those big dreams will begin to turn into your reality.

A Mantra for Being Imaginative

I dream big.

I dream big for myself.

I dream big for others.

I think about things differently.

I think about things creatively.

I think outside the box.

I push myself.

I am never satisfied.

There is no problem that I can't solve.

I am an innovative solutionist.

I initiate.

I take action.

I execute.

A SPACE TO DREAM BIG . . .

ATTRIBUTE FOUR

BE **PRESENT**

Being present means pausing and breathing
in the moment to bring oxygen to the brain and
stillness to the nervous system.
It means saying, "I'm here."

If you can't fly then run,
if you can't run then walk,
if you can't walk then crawl,
but whatever you do you have
to keep moving forward.

– MARTIN LUTHER KING JR.

ACTIVITY

Close your eyes and breathe for 30 seconds. How does that make you feel?

_____

_____

_____

_____

_____

_____

_____

_____

_____

BE PRESENT

∞ ○

THE WILLINGNESS TO KEEP SHOWING UP, DOING SOMETHING, AND LIVING WITH AN ATTITUDE OF PROGRESS AND NOT PERFECTION.

gsdfactor.com

KEEP SHOWING UP

In my life, there are a lot of areas where I have to focus on staying present and diligent. What helps is that as a creative problem solver, I've learned that I will never get it right the first time, but if I try, fail fast, try again, and keep showing up, I'll find power in the journey.

Showing up takes on many vantage points. Showing up for ourselves but also for others. My tiny human's karate school requires that even if you are not actively practicing on the mats, you still stand ready and present, showing up for your fellow teammates and cheering them on because sometimes just being there is enough. That's showing up too. Sometimes, all you have in you is to cheer on someone else, and when you can do that, you're showing up for that friend.

What happens when the odds are stacked against you? How do you keep showing up when it's feeling especially hard? As I discussed previously, I once returned to work after one of my maternity breaks to a hostile working environment that was clearly meant to isolate and antagonize me, and ultimately punish me for having had a baby. It was workplace harassment and adult bullying. At that time, I was faced with the option to show up or not. Even though my role and responsibilities were taken from me, I still showed up. I showed up for me, I showed up for other colleagues, but more importantly, I showed up for other working moms in my organization and in my industry. One of my favorite Instagram influencers, Alethea Crimmins (@ms_hdic), always signs off on her motivational nuggets with, "Be great in their face!" That's it in a nutshell.

Showing up even in the face of adversity or just meanness is a lesson that I'm already teaching my kids. Both my tiny humans have experienced and survived bullying in all its mediums, be it verbal, emotional, and/or physical. We taught our kids four steps that they could activate when they found themselves in these situations with their bully. When the bullying starts, take a deep breath and make sure you are in a safe space. Use your voice to defend yourself from the bully. Use your voice to escalate to a teacher or coach, and finally let it go. We have trained them in the art of martial arts, and they know how to defend themselves should the situation call for it, but in many cases, the bully is trying to bait you to retaliate to get you in trouble. By initially working these four basic steps, you don't fall into their trap. Now don't get me wrong, when the situation calls for it, defend yourself and handle it. Bullies can't stand when you keep showing up day after day, moment after moment. Keep showing up, keep amplifying, and keep being great in their face!

ACTIVITY

Reflect on if you have been the victim of bullying. How did you keep showing up? Is there anything you would have done differently?

_____

_____

_____

_____

_____

Now maybe some of you are the bully. Now is a time for you to reflect on your actions. Do you want to continue, or are you ready to make a change? Reflect on those that you bullied and how you would interact differently with them.

_____

_____

_____

_____

A SPACE TO DREAM BIG . . .

A SPACE TO DREAM BIG . . .

PROGRESS NOT PERFECTION

Attention GSDers! With all this talk about getting stuff done, it would be negligent of me not to warn you about one possible side-effect of GSDing. As you start building the motivation to be confident, imaginative, inquisitive, and now present, you might start feeling pressure to reach perfection.

First of all, what is perfection? I think of perfection as the expectation that mistakes are unallowable and unacceptable. The desire to want to perform to perfection or to create perfect outcomes is human and has its benefits, like seemingly flawless product and performance executions. It would seem that since I have already discussed the need to keep showing up, perfection would be the obvious reason why one would need to do so. That couldn't be farther from the truth. Be careful, GSDers, that you are not pressuring yourself to keep showing up in the pursuit of perfection. That's a slippery slope. Instead, I'd like to challenge you to embrace the concept of *progress, not perfection*.

This is a much better goalpost to target because it only requires you to be there. It's a given that anything you are doing will be excellent because you are already working on being confident, imaginative, and inquisitive. With attributes like that, the outcomes cannot be anything less than amazing. Perfectionism can be subtle, though, so make sure that you are exercising balance and setting realistic expectations when you show up. You do that by ensuring that you are constantly integrating rest and reevaluation into your routines. Know that being a work-in-progress is completely fine.

Sometimes, showing up means just that. You just have to BE. Sometimes, *being* looks well-put together, organized, and efficient. Other times, *being* looks broken and like a complete state of surrender, but the important part is that you are there. You are allowed to give yourself grace for those times. Perfectionists don't extend themselves grace. They don't celebrate the wins because the target is always moving. They are never satisfied, but not in the way that precipitates more knowledge and growth; they are never satisfied in a way that doesn't allow for a break or a self-congratulatory high-five. Resting and being in the moment are foreign concepts. This can lead to burnout, and I've been there.

ACTIVITY

Sometimes we think we have to do things perfectly to be successful, but that's not true. Rather than stress yourself to achieve perfection, focus on doing your best to complete your projects, tasks, or goals. Once you do finish, ask yourself these two questions:

1. Did I complete this to the best of my ability?

2. Am I proud of myself?

If you can answer those two questions with a yes, consider that a success.

Now you try. Think of the most recent goal, task, or project you had. Ask yourself those two questions and record the answers in the space below. If you answered "Yes," great. If you answered "No," write what you could have done differently to get a yes to those questions. Either way, don't beat yourself up about it. Use the experience to strive for better for the next challenge.

Did I complete this to the best of my ability?   _____ Yes _____ No

If no, what could you have done differently?

_____

_____

Am I proud of myself?   _____ Yes _____ No

If no, what could you have done differently?

_____

_____

I've also had to learn over time that effort and output can be managed. What do I mean by this? When I need to give 100%, then that's what I do. When I need to only give 80%, then that's what I do.

GSDers have a tendency to be individuals who can beautifully manage their effort and output, being selective as to when they can give 80% or 100%. They are also highly efficient and effective producers, which also means that a GSDer's 80% might be a non-GSDer's 100%. It's truly how we get so much stuff done.

It would be better for people who struggle with perfectionism to simply get good with good enough. Get good with leaving things for the next day. Get good with laying out your to do list or initiatives into three buckets of NOW, NEXT, and LATER. There will always be something.

We have begun tapping into the concept of "good enough", but for now, let's focus on progress. *Webster's Dictionary* defines progress as "forward or onward movement toward a destination." Progress means you keep showing up. You are doing something, anything. You are moving forward, even if it means a little. You just start even though you know it won't be the end result.

There are a couple of things you can do each day to make sure you keep moving forward. I've found that, as an entrepreneur, I need to make a few small, actionable steps each day, like maintaining consistent communication with the necessary parties, be it via emails or text messages. I make sure things are filed away properly and that my social media and other online content is up-to-date. Again, the goal is progress, not perfection, and progress means trusting the process while you prepare for the opportunities that are coming.

Now that we have discussed the importance of progress over perfection and the significance of making small, actionable steps each day, let's address the elephant in the room. What do we do when things are not going as planned? We go back to the basics. We go back to where we started, making little steps and progress each day. We lean all the way in. We are methodical. We set our intentions daily. We celebrate the little wins.

ACTIVITY

What are some of your back-to-basics activities that are specifically grounding for you?

_____

_____

_____

_____

_____

_____

A businesswoman friend of mine talks about how the founder's or leader's mindset is so critical and important to entrepreneurial success. The founder's mindset is the set of foundational beliefs that serve you throughout your life. Many times, leaders have to come back to this mindset when they need to reset and refocus:

This mindset includes:

- Influence

- Zone of mastery

- Asking for help

Your influence reminds you of what impact you make on society. In moments of stress, ask yourself, "What is my reach and influence?"

Then, think about your zone of mastery: what are the skill sets that you have and do well? What is your superpower? What have you mastered along the way? Often, when we are going back to the basics, we can lean into our zone of mastery because it's well-known and comfortable, and we are most confident doing those things.

Then finally, consider the art of asking for help. Learn to know when there is either a gap in your time and execution, your goals, or your skill sets. Believe that asking for help is a sign of strength and surrender. Even if you have a firm grasp on these ideas, you can be sure that you will still run into difficulties as a leader, specifically the temptation to be perfect. We must constantly remind ourselves that we are works in progress, and remember, it's *progression over perfection*.

ACTIVITY

Reflect on one area of your life where you tend to seek perfection. Identify specific, small, and consistent steps you can take to shift your focus towards progress, not perfection. Come back to this section periodically to track your progress.

A SPACE TO DREAM BIG . . .

BE PRESENT

My daughter plays softball, and one season, there weren't enough girls to make a team. Consequently, the coaches asked her if she wanted to join the boys' team. Without hesitation, she said, "Momma, you are the only girl on your work calls, and I want to be brave just like you. I want to play with the boys, and it's ok that I'm the solo girl on the baseball team." That comment hit me hard. What I realized was that she was watching. She was listening. She was observing. She was absorbing and taking bits and pieces of what she witnessed in my life and adapting them to her own life and experiences.

Remember: there are always eyes watching and ears listening.

Being present requires intentional awareness, and one way to be intentionally aware is to be an active listener. What does being an active listener mean? It's when you set intentions to hear the words, the purpose of the message, and the context surrounding it all. MindTools shares the following reasons that we listen:

- We listen to obtain information

- We listen to understand

- We listen for enjoyment

- We listen to learn

Another example of the importance of active listening is when you are receiving instructions. If your boss or instructor is giving you instructions for an assignment, and you only listen to the first part and start doing, you are likely going to miss some crucial steps to completing the task or, at the very least, completing it accurately. I often use this phrase: "Slow down to speed up." If we rush through the listening process, we are going to miss critical details, but if we slow down and hear all the information, when it is time to go, we will be able to finish at great speed.

Are you practicing and modeling active listening in your conversations and behavior? What if you were to make a conscious effort to be present with active listening? How could it transform your GSD Factor Life?

ACTIVITY

Share an example where you could leverage active listening in your life. Remember: Active listening requires more than just hearing. Pay attention to verbal and non-verbal cues. Listen to understand and not respond, and try not to interrupt.

A SPACE TO DREAM BIG . . .

A SPACE TO DREAM BIG . . .

PIVOT DECISIONS

My earliest memory of having to make a pivot decision, a decision that completely changed the trajectory of my life, started at the age of fifteen. I was on my way to a professional dance career with our local ballet company, training with some amazing dancers who would go on to perform on some of the most renowned national and international stages. Then I got sick, very sick. After being diagnosed with Lyme's disease two years later, I was quickly shifted from the pre-professional homeschool life, but I now had to get accustomed to what I would classify as a normal life. What was this thing called high school? I wasn't sure, but I decided to fully embrace my junior and senior years by taking advantage of whatever school had to offer. With this pivot, I fully immersed myself. I wanted to give the pivot every chance and opportunity to teach me something new, bring me joy, satisfaction, and fulfillment, and ultimately give me a chance to try things that I wouldn't have had time or availability to do in my pre-pivot life.

ACTIVITY

Name a time in which you experienced one of life's pivots. How did that pivot change the trajectory of your life or relevant situation? What did you learn from the pivot?

_____

_____

_____

_____

_____

_____

_____

_____

_____

_____

Some pivots in life present multiple lessons and nuggets, and it's important to lean into those lessons. Once my Lyme's disease was fully in remission, I was ready for my next pivot: co-founding a dance school. Just a year after opening up the dance school where I was feeding my love of dance by teaching and choreographing, life threw another curveball at me. This one would require me to have four knee surgeries over the course of eighteen months. Are you kidding me? I had lost dance once. I pivoted my dream to teaching and choreography, got back into dance shape, and was performing with my students, which was such an honor. And for what? For it to be taken again?

My late father always said I had to have a backup plan, just in case. He was a two-time Rose Bowl-winning quarterback with Stanford University, but he also experienced countless injuries, which hindered his professional career. Consequently, he pivoted to the Air Force. Knowing my dad's journey and personal pivots taught me that no matter what life throws at you, you can pivot. You can find the next thing that brings you joy, peace, satisfaction, and fulfillment.

For many years, I had to find other outlets besides dance; one of those outlets was coaching people. I love dreaming big with them. I live for the text message or call that says, "I have a problem. Can we chat?" I'm here for the good, bad, and tricky situations. I get joy from transforming words into people's plans or mapping out the steps into action. It feels good to know that I helped someone do something amazing, or gave them key actions, steps, and a plan for what to do next. It's like a puzzle. You can either start at all the edges and move in or start by finding the individual themes within and grouping them. You can approach it any way you want or the best way for your brain, but the ultimate goal is to finish the puzzle. I like being there to help put that puzzle together. If those circumstances with my health and my injuries hadn't happened, I would not be sitting where I am today. You would not be reading this book. Those events, and how I allowed them to mold and shape me, opened up opportunities for the future.

There are times in everyone's life when we come to a decision point or crossroads where it is clear that there are two paths or two choices. Those are the pivot moments that can lead to reinvention and a whole different set of opportunities. In these circumstances, one may have to answer questions such as: Should I go left or go right? Should I move forward, or should I stop? Should I remain satisfied, or keep pushing? These decisions can be scary because of the uncertainty, but they can also be hugely successful and impactful if navigated effectively.

A SPACE TO DREAM BIG . . .

ACTION PLAN

HOW TO BE PRESENT

Being present may seem like a more passive GSD attribute, but the reality is that being present involves a great deal of intentionality. Think about it. All of the sub-attributes in this section require constant consideration and adjustment of our perception. You cannot keep showing up, focusing on progress, not perfection, being present, or making pivot decisions if you are not consistently and intentionally thinking of doing all those things. The hardest part about consistently and intentionally being present by maintaining all four of these sub attributes is the risk of falling into perfectionism. If you find that you lean on the side of perfectionism, or you are a recovering perfectionist, here are some actionable steps you can take to be present without being a perfectionist.

1. Keep showing up. Create a list of small, go-to steps that will ensure you keep showing up, which means being present, even if for a moment. It's the art of doing something—anything, and trusting that process, even when it seems that there are more pivots than plans. Your small steps can include things like a daily gratitude journal or a check-in with a workout partner. Whatever the steps are, they will be unique to your lifestyle and should be tailored to whatever you need to keep you in a state of awareness to keep showing up.

2. Extend yourself grace. This is more of an informal step, but it's still important. Make sure you are reminding yourself that the focus is progress, not perfection, and that, therefore, you will mess up. You will make mistakes. The key is to accept wherever you are in your process, so that it's easier for you to commit to taking a step, any step, forward.

3. Celebrate your wins. As a recovering perfectionist, I now appreciate the fact that progress is good enough. Moving the needle, accomplishing one task, or doing one thing for ourselves should be celebrated. Take the time to do that. It can be as small as a verbal "Good job" to yourself, or as big as throwing a party when you reach your goals. Whatever the accomplishment, acknowledge it and celebrate it.

4. The commitment to being present requires a change in mindset, reminding us to be actively aware of recordings that are playing in our heads, and when our minds wander, we must reset, be it with meditation, music, or spoken word. Being present also means remembering one of the simplest of things—to breathe. I have a picture on my desk of two beautifully painted lungs that simply says, "Inhale, exhale." Bring it back to your breath. It will bring clarity. It will slow down your heart rate. It will steady the emotions. It will bring stillness to your nervous system.

Finally, being present requires an ever-present attitude of gratitude for progress, not perfection. It's great to get all the things done, but this attribute allows you to be grateful and accepting of the times when you don't.

A Mantra for Being Present

I am still.

I breathe in.

I am silent.

I breathe out.

I am present.

I am at peace.

I show up for me.

I show up for others.

I am enough.

I am a beautiful work in progress.

I move forward.

I am one with my breath.

I am exactly where I need to be.

A SPACE TO DREAM BIG . . .

A SPACE TO DREAM BIG . . .

ATTRIBUTE FIVE

BE **RESILIENT**

Being resilient means inhabiting a mental strength and superpower of perseverance in the face of doubt.

Hardships often prepare ordinary people for an extraordinary destiny.

– C.S. Lewis

ACTIVITY

Complete this sentence:

"I, _____ (Insert name here) am resilient.

I am a force to be reckoned with. I love myself. I am bold. I am brave.

I am brilliant. My voice is my strongest weapon."

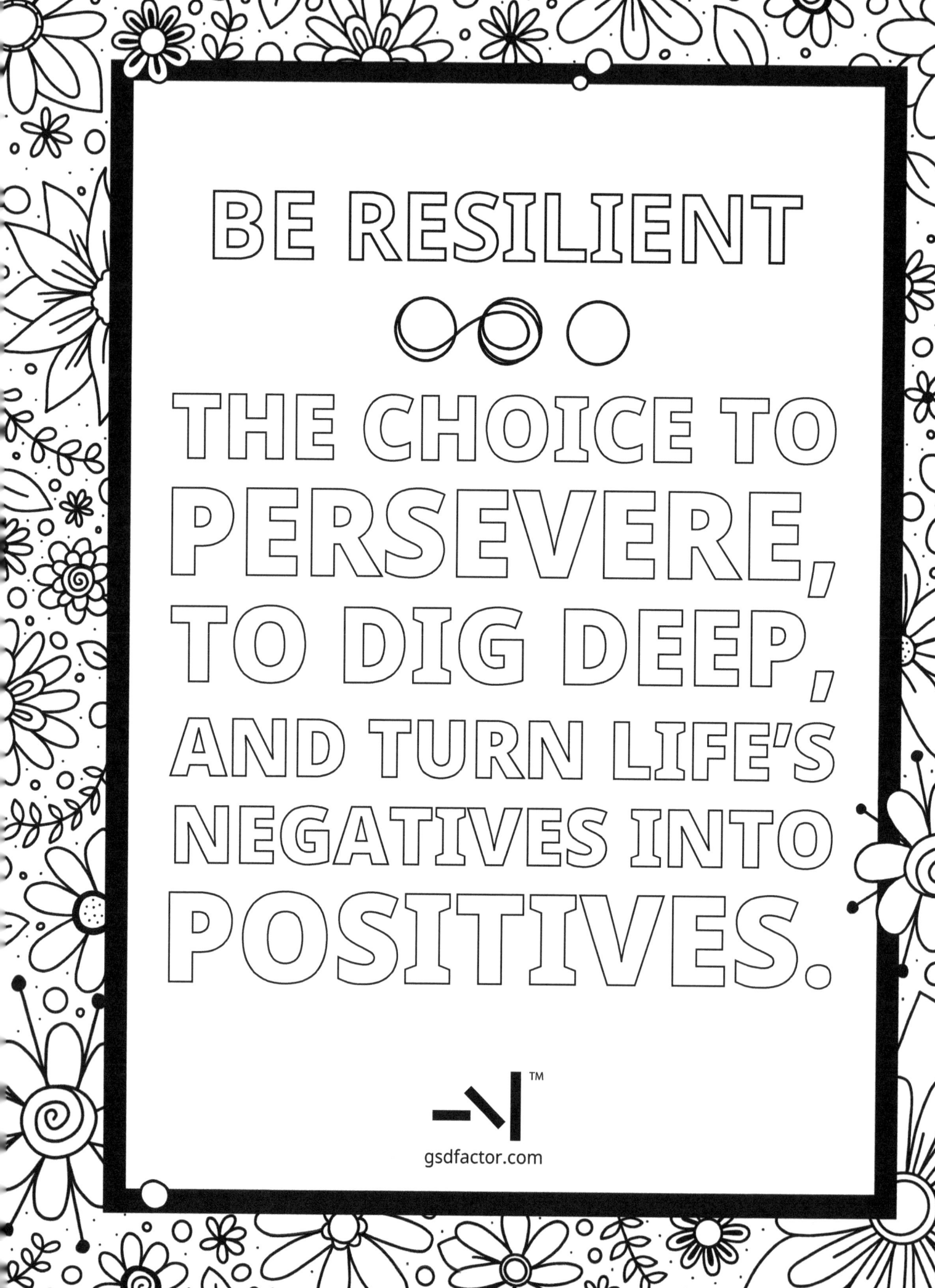

BE RESILIENT

THE CHOICE TO PERSEVERE, TO DIG DEEP, AND TURN LIFE'S NEGATIVES INTO POSITIVES.

gsdfactor.com

RESILIENT LIFE

Throughout this book, I've talked about the power of showing up, pivoting, and learning something from every situation. All these lessons are driving towards the GSD Factor attribute of being resilient.

Being resilient is about having an attitude that says life can be tough, with days that are good and days that are bad, but the sun rises in the morning.

Resilience requires honest acknowledgment of where you are. In order to be resilient, you have to be authentic with yourself and your current circumstances. Part of being resilient is knowing that when you are knocked down, it's okay to sit, cry, yell, scream, or do whatever you need to do in that moment. Those feelings need to get out. We are human, and we all feel things. That's how we were created. Resilience is not pushing down those feelings of sadness or anger but holding them, honoring them, and then letting them go. We hold space for them for as long as they still serve us. We are present with them as long as it takes to get it out of our system. That's what you need, but then, you rise from the ashes. You get back up.

Think about a loss you have experienced in your life or a traumatic event or situation that robbed you of something. Have you given yourself permission to grieve it? Have you even talked about it? I have found, in these moments, that the sooner I talk, cry, yell, or scream out my frustrations, the sooner my head, heart, and emotions all come back into alignment to be present and face the grief, sorrow, anger, and injustice head-on.

For those of you who aren't comfortable talking with others about what you're facing, just start writing. Grab a journal, and start writing without thinking. Let the words flow out of you—every thought, frustration, anger, sorrow, joy, and any other emotion you're feeling. By speaking—or writing—these words out, we acknowledge them and acknowledge what's happening. Only then can we move forward and be in action. It's then that we can begin to be resilient.

ACTIVITY

Reflect on a challenging experience you have gone through and how you have grown from it. What feelings come up as you are thinking and writing? Have you talked to someone about it?

_____

_____

_____

_____

_____

_____

_____

_____

_____

_____

Athletes are some of the best at showing us how to live life with resilience. They often reflect on wins and losses. They study footage and tape to see what they did wrong so they can learn and not make the same mistake again. In business, we call this process "retrospect." It's during this time that we ask the tough questions. What went wrong? What could we have done better, and what can we do better moving forward?

Applying the process of retrospecting to life will help you see that we never reach a finished level while living a resilient life. Resilience is one of those things upon which we can continue to grow and improve. It's one of the first lessons we learn when we are born, and it can be one of the final lessons before you move on from this life. Each day can be a lesson in resilience. Each time you find yourself in a circumstance asking, "What can I learn from this? What can I learn to do versus not to do?" recognize that that's you exercising your resilience muscle. That's how you grow and expand your resilience and stamina. The next time something comes up, an experience with bullying or harassment, an illness, a hard project, the loss of someone or something you love, whatever it is, your resilience muscle memory will kick in, and it will become a little easier to bounce back.

Being resilient is the GSD Factor attribute and life skill of knowing that even though we have to go through things in life, we can learn something, and we can help somebody else by sharing that lesson. As we walk out on that journey, it becomes a part of our story. A story that can be shared with others. A story that brings change. A story that brings hope.

ACTIVITY

Think of moments of resilience that you have experienced in your life. Now gather a small container, such as a shoe box or jar. Create a time capsule that represents your journey of resilience. You can include objects, notes, drawings, or any other meaningful items that symbolize your resilience, such as quotes, photos, or mementos. Afterward, share what you included in your time capsule and why, reflecting on your resilient experiences and the significance of the items you chose.

(This exercise works even if you don't have a container or immediate access to all the physical objects. Imagine you have access to everything, what would you include and why?)

_____

_____

_____

_____

_____

_____

_____

_____

A SPACE TO DREAM BIG . . .

A SPACE TO DREAM BIG . . .

TRUST THE TIMING

Much of what we've discussed as it pertains to the GSD Factor attributes and sub attributes has been dependent on parts of our lives that we can control. You can control how you show up in the world by being confident. You can control how much you know by being inquisitive. You can control how you handle problems by being imaginative and how you react to life's curveballs by being present. Being resilient also has an element of personal control in that you have to make a choice to continue to get up after being knocked down, but there is an element of uncertainty that exists within this GSD Factor attribute that doesn't necessarily show up in others: timing. No matter how confident, inquisitive, imaginative, or present we are in any situation, if the timing isn't right, it's not happening. That's what makes resilience so important and sometimes challenging. Being resilient also means being aware that we cannot control timing, but we must trust it.

What does it look like to trust the timing? Though we can't control timing, we aren't just passively experiencing time. So let's talk about how we manage the time we have. When you look at your life with work, family, friends, events, or activities, you probably have to juggle and make sure there is enough time for all of it.

Regardless of all the responsibilities you may have, you have to take care of yourself first. Consider this: what we give to others comes from what we give to ourselves. Furthermore, if we haven't made time to give ourselves rest, love, grace, patience, etc., where are we going to find it to give to others? Your family, your team, your friends, and you—yes, even *you*—are all counting on you. If you aren't able to be there, those things don't function the way they are intended to function. Now, that doesn't mean that you can't ever not be there. It means that if you are not there, it should not be as a result of your lack of self-care. Managing our time to include self-care requires balance. That's the real issue. Remember, we are striving for work-life-family integration–and that includes self-care.

ACTIVITY

Recount an experience in which timing affected your life. Looking back on that experience, are you grateful for how things happened? Why or why not?

_____

_____

_____

_____

_____

_____

_____

_____

_____

_____

When you evaluate your workload, think about what progress, not perfection, looks like. I'm always evaluating what needs to be done, and I always have a list. One of my employees shared that she categorizes her personal and professional life into three buckets:

- NOW – These are the items that need to be addressed immediately. You might get to them today or tomorrow, but getting them done is critical.

- NEXT – These are the items that may be completed tomorrow or this week. They are a close follower after the "now" items but aren't the most pressing.

- LATER – These are the items that you have a little more time to ideate and plan. They could be addressed next week, next month, or next quarter, etc.

When your to-do list is categorized and prioritized, it's time to look at your responsibility pie. Imagine a pie, and create pieces of your pie for your work-life-family components. Are the right percentages represented? If work is 50% of your life, does the pie represent 50%? Furthermore, does it align with your to-do list for work items with realistic expectations? The other things to be mindful of are not only the responsibilities that you do have but the responsibilities you should have. So many times, we have responsibilities in our pie that should never have been ours to carry for any period of time. This is not to be confused with caring and taking care of others. This is truly remembering your boundaries and the boundaries of others and deciding to take what is yours to carry and what you can give back to others what was theirs to carry.

This last bit is worth repeating. Remember your boundaries and responsibilities and the boundaries and responsibilities of others. What are yours to carry? You keep these. What are theirs to carry? Give them back!

ACTIVITY

Think about the tasks in your life that you need to complete. List out your top 3 Now, Next, and Later tasks.

NOW

1. _____

2. _____

3. _____

NEXT

1. _____

2. _____

3. _____

LATER

1. _____

2. _____

3. _____

However you decide to group your long to-do list, and whatever timing buckets you use, just know that your entire list doesn't all have to be completed today and that you may not be able to do it all alone. Ask for help. Along with admitting that I'm not the smartest person in the room, I also remind myself that I'm not expected to get it all done today. We must remember to extend ourselves grace.

I know what you're thinking. Time management is great. Getting help is awesome, but what happens when life starts throwing curveballs? Well, that's when we have to learn to trust the timing. Athletes and dancers have an incredible sense of timing – timing of movements, timing of breathing, timing of sequence.

Let's use football as an example: Reading the defense in football is much like reacting to the challenges and uncertainties of life. Sure, there may be a plan, but maybe life is throwing us something for which we weren't prepared, forcing us to call an audible. An audible is a football term for when the quarterback has already given the offense a play in the huddle, but right before it's time to execute, the quarterback senses a shift in the defense's strategy. As a result, the quarterback makes an executive decision to change plays to face this new strategy. That happens all the time in real life. We make plans as well as we can, and suddenly, life shifts those plans. Then, like quarterbacks, we have to pause, re-evaluate, and re-execute.

In keeping with the football analogy, I can say that throughout my life, there have been many instances where the defense blitzed, executing a sudden and intense attack, causing me to call an audible. In some cases, I had to pause, re-evaluate, and re-execute. Life has taught me the importance of being agile. By looking at the past, retrospectively, I can see how it prepared me for the future.

Get good with change. Change is healthy. Change means that you are growing and evolving.

When you are thinking through strategic timing, you must have a vision that is fueling that passion. That vision is your map. Even when the timing seems off, or the strategy needs to be changed, your vision remains. Part of having that solid vision is having the foundation of knowing who you are and what you want out of life. That is your compass. That is your constant.

Perhaps another lesson to be learned from trusting the timing is whether your vision can stand the pressure of the seasons of uncertainty. Can your vision stand the test of time? Can it stand adversity? Can it stand the failures and successes? When timing and vision are being challenged or refined, that is a great opportunity to determine whether you should be in a state of doing or a state of being. Ask yourself, "Do I need to push or pull during this period?" Only you truly know what you need as you are walking out your journey. Trusting the timing is an important part of this attribute, because it also requires you to trust yourself. You have to trust in your own management of the time you have been given, and trust that you have prepared as much as you possibly can for those unexpected twists and turns of life. No matter how many times you get knocked down, trust the timing. Trust yourself and get back up. Eventually, you'll walk right into your success.

Along with trusting the timing, remember there are seasons of DOing and seasons of BEing. It is assumed that GSDers are always DOing, but in reality, we must have *seasons* of BEing to be able to balance out our *seasons* of DOing. Just like our bodies and brain need to rest and recharge, seasons of BEing allow our body, mind, soul, and emotions to rest and recharge, preparing for the next season of DOing. Your next season of DOing may require more out of you than ever before, so trust the timing and trust that the universe is giving you the season and tools you need for now and for the next chapter. Whichever season you are in, be all there and be present.

ACTIVITY

We're going to prepare timelines. For this first timeline, mark important life moments, events, challenges, and achievements. Reflect on how past experiences, both good and bad, have shaped your journey and prepared you for the future.

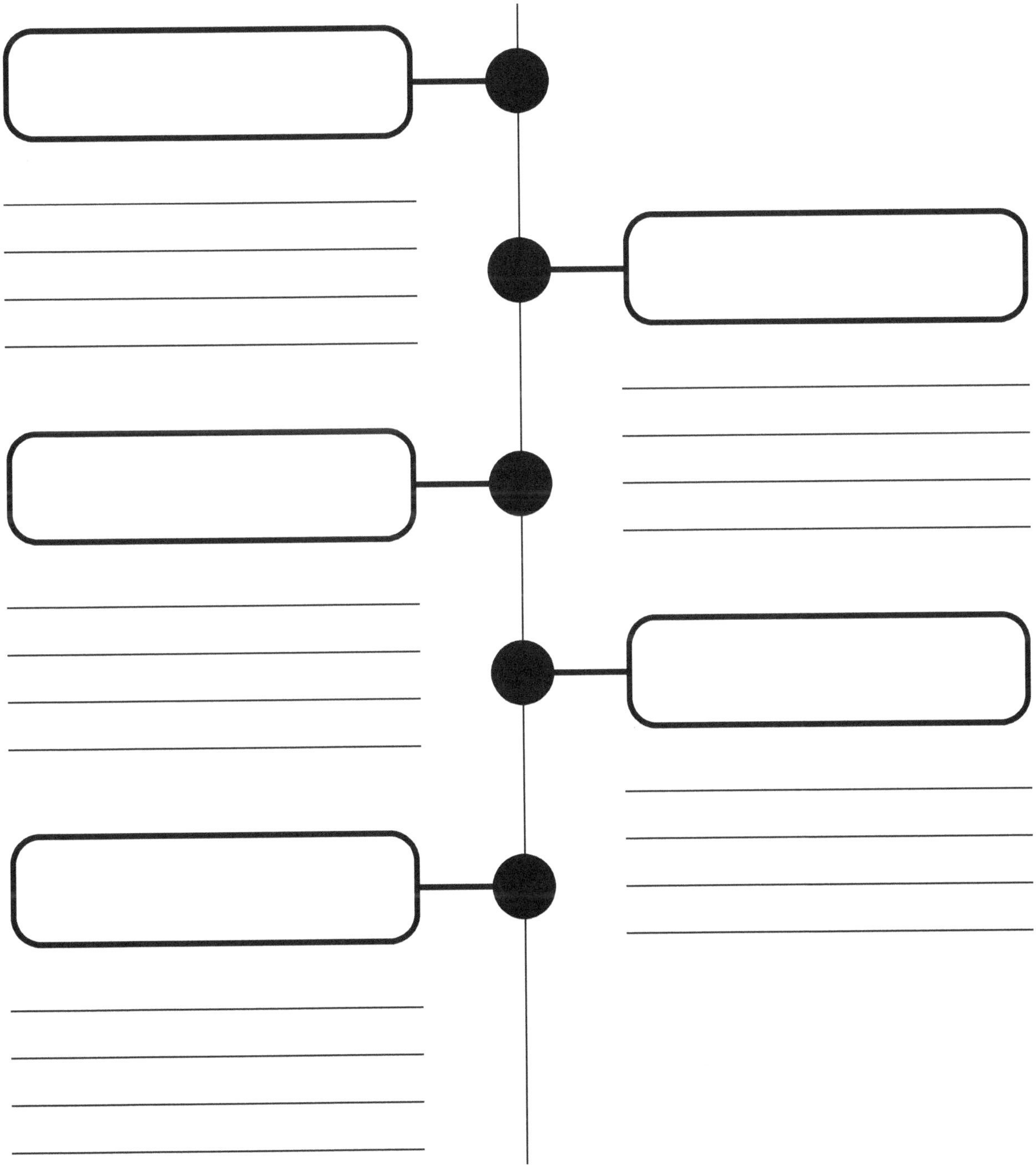

The second timeline is of your future. Consider that there may be many challenges, detours and situations that pop up along the way. Also consider that those future experiences will help mold and shape you the same way the experiences in your past have molded you up until now.

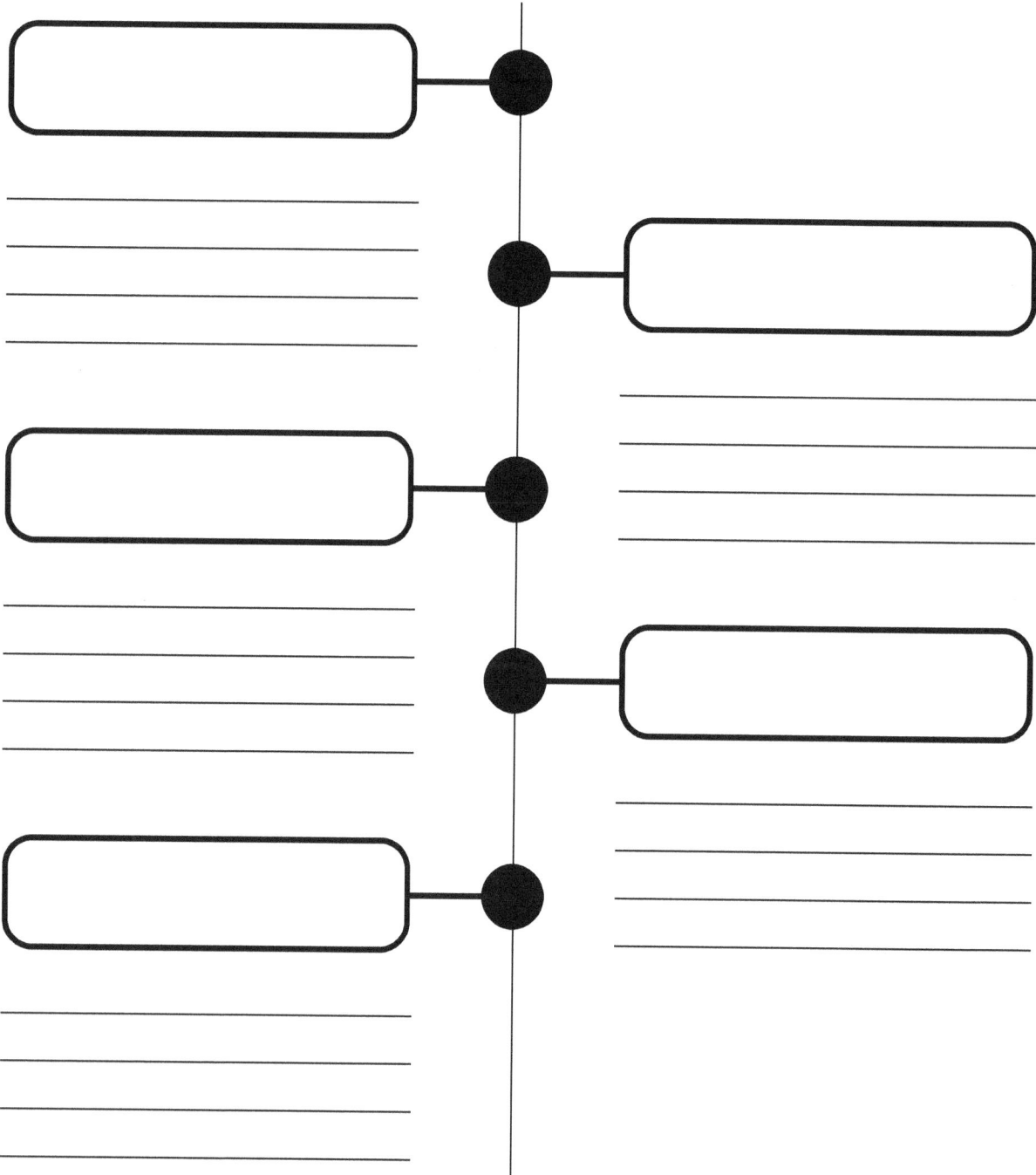

A SPACE TO DREAM BIG . . .

A SPACE TO DREAM BIG . . .

PERSPECTIVE

Have you ever met or known someone whose presence can brighten up the room they walk into? They offer a different point of view on things, large or small. I call them "breath-of-fresh-air" people. These people provide balance by providing another way to look at things.

Perspective is the way we see life and the experiences it brings. Perhaps you have had a tough time in life with your family or your health. That daily battle can bring perspective or perseverance like nothing else. It cuts through the stuff and forces you to see and acknowledge what truly matters. Perspective lessons at any young age shape you, mold you.

To those of you who are, perhaps, on a journey where you have to exercise your perseverance every day, I see you. I hear you. I'm cheering you on. Your GSD community is cheering you on. Your ability to be resilient is directly related to how you see the struggles and challenges you may face. I challenge you to consider the concept of perspective lessons the next time you find yourself in a difficult situation. It may be hard, but think about how much wiser you are going to be on the other side. Don't let it rattle you. You've got this.

ACTIVITY

I call this activity, the Glass Half-Full Exercise. Think about a situation in your life that didn't go exactly how you would have wanted. Write in the top of the jar what didn't go right and write in the bottom of the jar what did go right.

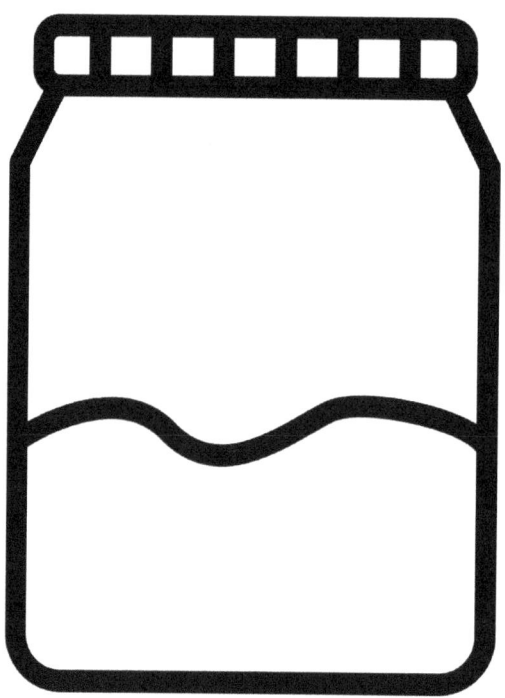

Then complete the sentence below to help you see that situation with a more positive perspective.

_____ didn't go as I would have liked,

but _____

Here's an example:

    I didn't get the promotion, but interviewing gave me more confidence to share my story and helped me figure out what I really want to be doing.

A SPACE TO DREAM BIG . . .

ACTION PLAN

HOW TO BE RESILIENT

Living out a resilient life takes sheer will. It requires grit. It requires you to dig deep. Resilience requires the stamina and perseverance to acknowledge that life can be tough sometimes, but also leaves room to acknowledge the moments for learning and growth.

I had the opportunity to hear former First Lady Michelle Obama speaking at Salesforce's Dreamforce. She was calling those of us in the room to be better people. To use our voices. To stand up for what is right. But she acknowledged that life will knock you down and that the best way to respond is, "When they go low, you go high." We've all heard her say this; it's probably her most famous quote. She first shared it at the 2016 Democratic National Convention. But to hear those words first-hand, while standing in the same room as her, illuminated how a little mantra like this can shift our perspective and create resilience. That's it. It's that simple. "When they go low, you go high." This concept is so easy to remember. So easy to understand. I've taught my tiny humans this same lesson, especially as they have walked out their individual bullying stories.

Many times, people will ask me for advice on how to be resilient. It's no simple process, but in attempting to reduce resilience to a series of actionable items, I suggest several things:

- Take time to feel your feels. You are a human, not a robot. Sometimes you need to get that raw emotion out.

- Keep a level-headed mindset, one that is open to seeing your situation from a different perspective. Remember those perspective lessons, and try to remain aware that whatever the situation is, there may be another way to look at it and learn.

- Ensure that as you experience hardship, you remain present in body, mind, soul, and emotion. No matter what hardships you are experiencing, you can still experience joy, happiness, and love in those challenging times as well, as long as you stay present and open to it.

Be sure to maintain your perspective by walking with humility and gratitude. Think about what you will be able to share with others at the end of this journey. Be grateful that you made it to the other side and are able to share the wisdom you have gained. Think about how this weaves itself into your story. You are extraordinary. You are resilient. You are destined for great things.

A Mantra for Being Resilient

I am resilient.

I matter.

I am a force to be reckoned with.

I love myself.

I am bold.

I am brave.

I am brilliant.

My voice is my strongest weapon.

I am courageous.

I am valiant.

I am strong.

I am extraordinary.

I am destined for great things.

A SPACE TO DREAM BIG . . .

ATTRIBUTE SIX

BE **INFLUENTIAL**

Being influential means being a leader.
It's about knowing when to listen and when to act.

> If you want to change the world, start with yourself.
>
> – Mahatma Gandhi

ACTIVITY

List the top five characteristics you think a good leader should have.

_____

_____

_____

_____

_____

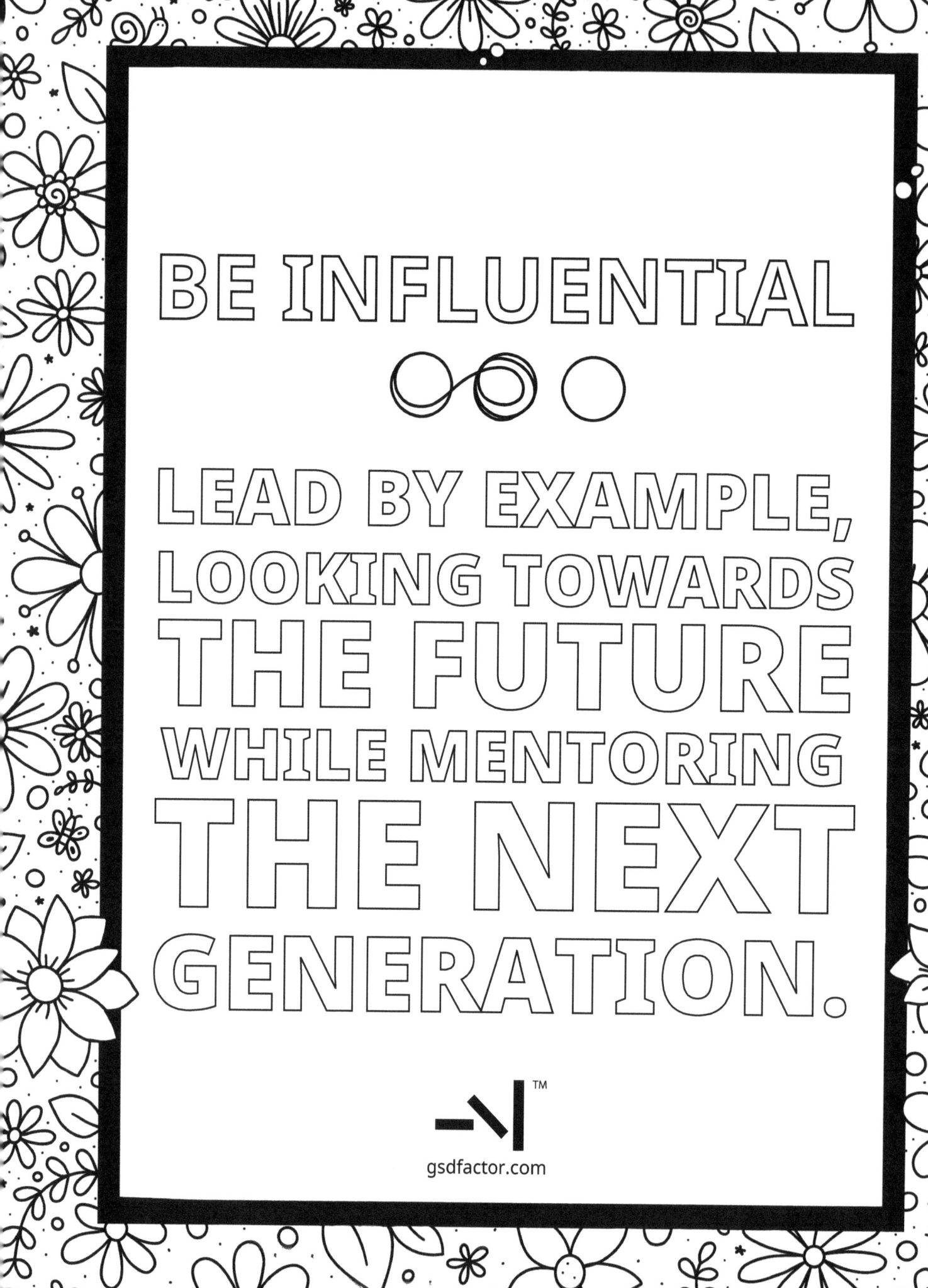

BE INFLUENTIAL

LEAD BY EXAMPLE, LOOKING TOWARDS THE FUTURE WHILE MENTORING THE NEXT GENERATION.

gsdfactor.com

LEADER BY EXAMPLE

What does being a leader mean to you? There are countless examples of leadership all around us: good leaders, bad leaders, young leaders, old leaders, leaders who had great wisdom, and leaders who didn't make the best decisions. To me, being a leader is about knowing when to listen and when to act. It's about showing up. GSD Factor leaders are present and authentic. They know when they need to lead, when to follow, when to push, and when to support.

Organizations have varying levels of leaders—inspirational leaders, visionary leaders, and imaginative, innovative solutionist leaders. All three are important, and the type of leader determines the culture of the company/organization. Inspirational leaders lead through motivation and appeal to the humanity of their teams. Visionary leaders are those who can easily see how to take a company from level to level and into the future. They're always looking for the opportunity to take a calculated risk and watch it pay off. Finally, we have innovative solutionist leaders. They are the drivers of change. They aim to be the first and break the mold. Organizations need people like that to find solutions and create new, better processes.

Some leaders are called in to solve and fix specific problems. They might also be needed to mediate a particular situation or to turn an organization around and save it from its downfall. No matter what kind of leader you are, one thing remains. Being a leader is hard and lonely at times. Leaders have to make tough decisions. When you are assigned this task, first actively listen to all parties, taking into consideration their views or thoughts. Now, armed with information from both sides, you will have to make the best decision with the information you have at that moment considering everyone involved. Decisions like this may or may not be popular, but this isn't a popularity contest. It's a character-building exercise that is training you on the art of being a leader.

ACTIVITY

What is the toughest decision you have had to make?

_____

_____

_____

_____

What was the outcome of that decision? Do you still think your choice was right? Why or why not?

_____

_____

_____

_____

There are examples of leaders all around us, but there are a couple that I've been especially impressed with. Jacinda Ardern, the former prime minister of New Zealand, was a trailblazer in many ways, including being the world's youngest female head of government and taking her baby to a United Nations meeting. After leading New Zealand through the terror attack in Christchurch and the unprecedented COVID-19 pandemic, she stepped down when she knew her tank was empty. True leaders know when to step up and take over, but they also know when to hand the reins over to someone who can continue their progress and further build upon their accomplishments.

Will.i.am is not only a renowned rapper and producer, but he is a leading technology entrepreneur who is shaking things up. He is a strong advocate for human intelligence and investing intentionally in our youth and communities. He is challenging the technology industry with creating new ways to address the world's most pressing problems and leveraging technology to provide innovative solutions.

Whitney Wolfe Herd, former founder and CEO of Bumble Inc., is the world's youngest self-made female billionaire and the youngest woman to take a company public. She did all this and more within a year of having a baby. Not only has she served millions of women around the world with her company and offerings, but she's also shown that women can do it all*: have a career, be successful, and be a new mom.

* I'm careful of overgeneralizing this phenomenon. I realize that "doing it all" or "having it all" means different things to different women. For Whitney, it was running a company, taking it public (ringing the stock exchange bell with her baby on her hip!), being a mom, and much more. For me, it's creating a work-life-family integration that balances my aspirations, entrepreneurial spirit, and my family. For you, it might be working full-time while taking a course part-time and being a caregiver to an elderly parent. Doing or having it all can be whatever *you* want it to be.

ACTIVITY

Who are some leaders that you are inspired by? Are they inspirational leaders, visionary leaders, or imaginative, innovative solutionist leaders?

_____

_____

_____

_____

_____

_____

_____

_____

_____

_____

Being a leader calls for a level of courage like no other. Sometimes, it means standing in for your team or colleagues. Sometimes, it even means mustering your courage to stand in front of bullies and defend the underdog.

For those who are aspiring to be leaders, we need you. We need leaders who walk with authentic conviction, who actively listen, and who have empathy. We need leaders who know when and how to take action, who can encourage and empower, and who seek equality. We need leaders who give back to their communities. We need leaders who are thinking about the next generation and preparing those future leaders to stand on their predecessors' shoulders. Remember, leadership is not for the faint of heart. It has its challenges, but it is also so rewarding.

The biggest lessons I've learned from being a leader are conviction and confidence in my decisions and my willingness to exhibit humility. When I make a decision, I do so unapologetically. I stick to it no matter the peer pressure I may receive. When I say no, it is a full sentence, and I do so without apology. However, I'm willing to acknowledge when I have made a mistake or something has gone awry. I'm a human, and therefore, I'm not impervious to making mistakes.

My goal as a leader has always been to stand up and protect those under me, whether they were employees, team members, or family; I am their advocate. I make sure I show up for them in the way they need me to show up for them. Whether it's an in-person coffee or lunch to prepare them for a big meeting, a text exchange with words of encouragement, or an after-work cocktail to decompress a situation and plan for how to react the following day.

Being a leader, at times, calls for pushing your team to excellence or raising them to the next level of growth. Effective leadership means pushing your team, rolling up your sleeves, and saying, "What can I do to help?" Be the leader by getting in the trenches to help, support, and encourage.

It's important to note that showing up for someone can be something quite small, or something large-scale. I've had many conversations with aspiring leaders who worry about their capacity to "show up." This is your reminder that showing up means simply that. Show up with your full attention and ability to listen with intention, and provide guidance from your own experience and wisdom.

ACTIVITY

What leadership traits do you already have?

_____

_____

_____

_____

_____

What traits do you want to develop to be a better leader in the future?

_____

_____

_____

_____

What are three, concrete steps you can take now to start developing those traits?

A SPACE TO DREAM BIG . . .

CHALLENGING THE STEREOTYPES

Have you ever been misunderstood or experienced having someone make a wrong assumption about you? This can be a very lonely and painful place. Someone's thoughts or perceptions of you are not the true picture of who you are. Oftentimes, people think they know best, and they think they can tell what kind of person someone is by their clothes, how they walk, or what they say. This simply isn't true.

My first challenge to you is this: don't judge a book by its cover. Take a moment to pause, then introduce yourself so that you are getting first-hand information. Then, ask questions, but more importantly, listen. You will be amazed at what you can learn. You never know—you may be surprised to meet a new friend.

My second challenge to you is to continue to be your true, authentic self. You may win some friends and lose some friends, but remember, no one can be *everyone's* friend. Surround yourself with positive, happy people that align with your life principles. You are a GSDer, someone who gets stuff done with confidence, inquisitiveness, imagination, presence, resilience, and influence, and who doesn't worry about what people think. Live your unicorn life.

I've shared that I've always lived that unicorn life of being unapologetically my true, authentic self. I looked up to individuals who always did things differently and especially found inspiration from women who were living out work-life-family integration by "having it all," whatever that specifically meant to them. For my 40th birthday, I purchased a hat for the first time ever. I loved how unique this Gigi Pip hat was; it exuded strength and femininity, yet what sold me was the interior ribbon that said, "For the woman who wears many hats." Additionally, what this brand stood for and how it is reshaping the female hat industry was very GSD Factor-like, and, therefore, I have become a Gigi Pip ambassador. I decided very quickly that my Gigi Pip hat would become part of my brand. You'll find me wearing it wherever and whenever I'm showing up and representing The GSD Factor Life, knowing that my typical industries of Insurance and Technology are not typically hat places. In fact, within the insurance world, there is only one other hat-wearing cohort, Tony Canas, who wears a top hat. He has fully embraced it and wears it, literally, around the world. Now, we have become hat buddies in our insurance world, and you can always find us in any room! Because of my consistency, as I run into people from event to event, they will now flag me down to say hello and exchange small conversations. They remember me because I'm the GSD hat lady. One female CEO said to me, "You have balls to wear that hat to industry events like this ... and I think it's awesome! It makes you memorable."

We often hear about building our personal brands; being or doing something that makes us stand out. I get a lot of questions about how to build a personal brand. Whatever your personal brand is, it has to be unique to you. And the most important aspect is that it needs to be authentically you. If your personal brand isn't in line with your core, authentic self, it will feel fake, and it may do more damage to your brand than simply being who you authentically are.

ACTIVITY

What are some stereotypes you think people may assume you fit? How have you challenged those stereotypes?

_____

_____

_____

_____

_____

_____

_____

_____

Think about your personal brand: What stands out about you, is unique to you, and can help others immediately identify you?

A SPACE TO DREAM BIG . . .

HEROES + SHEROES + MENTORS

We should always be showing gratitude and thanks for the mentors and heroes in our lives. Hopefully, we all have heroes and mentors, those that have inspired us. These are the people who have impacted us, who have seen something special in us when we did not see it in ourselves. I have been blessed with many of these people throughout my life.

The first shero I want to thank is someone I call my Warrior Princess. Her energy was amazing. When we met, we found an immediate synergy—a sisterly bond in empowering women of our varying generations. Our visions and our dreams were aligned. She was what some might call a jack of all trades. She was an artist, musician, entrepreneur, mentor, and leader who had a heart for investing in her community, specifically into other African-American women. To put it lightly, she was a powerhouse. It was like she saw no limits. She dreamed even bigger than I do, and that's saying a lot.

My next great mentor is my Fairy Godmother who helped my career trajectory and was a critical piece to my transition from a small business into the corporate world. She was a trailblazing recruiter in the Nashville area and was one of the founding members of a staffing company that went on to gain national renown. She redefined how you recruit someone but also how you recruit for them. She considered herself an advocate who needed to get to know the candidates in order to come along beside them, tell their stories, and get them placed in a career. She looked at a girl and saw the potential woman I could be. She saw my big personality that just got stuff done, and she said, "YES! I can use that."

From her perspective and seat as a recruiter, she could mold me, train me, and prepare me. Fairy Godmother started by teaching me the STAR methodology and how it applies to answering questions. These questions could be for job interviews or general problem solving:

STATE the situation.

List out the TASKS.

Explain the ACTION items.

Share the RESULTS.

And finally, during the writing of my *GSD Factor Teen Workbook,* I learned that heaven gained another one of my angel sheroes who I considered to be a spiritual mother. She had a profound impact on my personal life these last seventeen years. Her wisdom and spiritual guidance guided me through many of life's milestones. She was steadfast and faithful in her check-ins and encouragement even as her health faltered.

I share this as an encouragement to reach out to your heroes, sheroes, and mentors in your life to thank them. Be intentional and be present; let them hear from you. Share with them the impact they have made on your life.

ACTIVITY

Who is a mentor in your life and why?

_____

_____

_____

_____

_____

Have you told them? If not, why?

_____

_____

_____

_____

_____

Write a letter of gratitude to one of your heroes/mentors for the role they have played in your life. It doesn't have to be long or fancy, but consider sharing it with them one day.

_____

_____

_____

_____

_____

_____

_____

_____

_____

_____

_____

_____

If you don't yet have a mentor, take some time to think about the people in your life who may be good mentors, especially those who seem to have some of the same qualities you think a good leader should have. This may feel a little uncomfortable to you, but if you already have a relationship with any of these people, consider asking them if they would be willing to share some of their wisdom and expertise with you. If you don't know them, don't yet have a relationship with them, or are not yet comfortable asking for that level of guidance right now, consider researching some historical or well-known figures who may have or had leadership qualities you admire. There may be biographies or memoirs of their lives that will be informative and inspiring concerning how to be influential.

A SPACE TO DREAM BIG . . .

ACTION PLAN

HOW TO BE A LEADER

With my therapist, I find word clouds to be an extremely helpful exercise, and during the writing of this workbook, I had a session where this exercise came up. The three words that came to me were empowerment, resilience, and strength. What I think is so powerful about these three words is that they build on one another, and they are all traits of a leader. We must be empowered to be confident to achieve greatness. We must be resilient to stand up against anything or anyone that doesn't align. Finally, we must exhibit strength in our words and our actions.

As a leader and a GSDer, challenge injustice, give voice to the under-voiced, and stand for equality. While bringing along the next generation, honor those who have gone before you—your mentors, your heroes and your sheroes. Thank them for paving the way. Identify what kind of leader you want to be or aspire to be and do that. Live that. Find a mentor who speaks to your true, authentic self and who makes courage resonate within you. Above all, be who YOU are and get stuff done. That's it. It's that simple.

A Mantra for Being Influential

I am a leader.

I am bold.

I am courageous.

I am brave.

I amplify.

I lift up.

I push.

I support.

I speak with truth.

I speak with respect.

I listen.

I honor.

I am humble.

A SPACE TO DREAM BIG . . .

A SPACE TO DREAM BIG . . .

THE GSD FACTOR LIFE

My new favorite podcast is #HypeWomen hosted by Erin Gallagher. Each episode ends with her asking the guests to fill in the blanks:

I was...

I am...

I will be…

It's fascinating how each guest responds differently, some with very short answers, others with paragraphs. Each time I listen, I find myself pondering how I would answer that same question if asked:

I was *underestimated*.

I am *transforming*.

I will *fly*.

As a visual learner, I started to think about how this would look in picture or art form. To me, "I was underestimated" reminds me of a caterpillar. "I am transforming" reminds me of a chrysalis, and "I will fly" reminds me of a butterfly. This natural metamorphosis is a beautiful way to think about our own journey in life, be it professional or personal. Sometimes, we have to be encased in discomfort to become who we're meant to be and to achieve what we're capable of achieving.

Where are you on your journey? Are you in your caterpillar, chrysalis, or butterfly stage?

Recently, I was watching *Frozen 2* with my tiny humans, and the song "Show Yourself" seemed to speak to me like never before. The whole premise of the song basically asserts that whatever it is that you are looking for to give you validation or permission to succeed can only be found in you. You are the answer to your questions. You are the one you have been waiting for. That's what I want you to take away from this workbook.

All of the attributes we've discussed in this workbook—being Confident, Inquisitive, Imaginative, Present, Resilient, and Influential—are all parts of The GSD Factor Life.

I have told you what worked for me, the attributes that I found to have encouraged and transformed me, but ultimately, the action behind each attribute is your responsibility. You have to do the work for yourself. You have to show up. You have to decide which tools you are adding to your toolbox.

Being a GSDer will cause others to look to you for guidance. It is inevitable. Because once all these attributes are working in your life, people are going to notice that you get stuff done. Then, they are going to start watching you and maybe even asking you how you do it.

Here is my final challenge for you: How can you apply these attributes to your life?

You may decide after reading this that you are good with where you are, and that is okay. However, I hope that after reading this, and working through the activities, there is something inside you saying, "I want to get stuff done." When that happens, know that you've got this. You are not alone. You have taken that first step to say, "I am here. Hear my voice. Know my name. Watch as I write history for the next generation. Witness my story, my journey."

Now, let's get stuff done!

A SPACE TO DREAM BIG . . .

A SPACE TO DREAM BIG . . .